Praise for
The 100-Year PR Plan

The 100-Year PR Plan: A Guide for Advocates by Benjamin Miller is a fascinating manifesto on how non-profit organizations can 'be the change'. It is based on Miller's creative adaptation of the work of Quentin Skinner on conceptual change in the history of Western political thought. Over many decades Skinner has developed an exceptionally influential way of, first, understanding the ways in which political theorists engage in the activities of trying to change the normative conventions of the age in which they live, and second, of studying how successful and unsuccessful these attempts have been in the immediate context and in the longer term. Miller has studied this method thoroughly and redesigned it so it can used by non-profit organizations to work to bring about social change more effectively, and to learn by trial and error cycles to improve their techniques as they go along. It is an original and must-read contribution to the literature on non-profit organizations and on the "diffusion of innovations" literature more broadly.

—James Tully, Professor Emeritus, University of Victoria

This thoughtful, engaging, and practical book offers both an explanation for why words create changes in the world and how we might better find ways of making change happen through language. This is not a simple, professional how-to manual; it is a robust intellectual account of ideological transformation and how to make and re-make meaning based on the intellectual work of Quentin Skinner. The stakes are high when we are able to effectively manage and drive the kinds of change that Benjamin Miller describes, and all sorts of organizations can benefit from learning the methods in this book. With a plethora of examples to draw from, readers will surely find unique insights into why and how they might become better public communicators.

—Dr. Robert Danisch, Associate Professor and Chair, Department of Communication Arts, University of Waterloo

THE
100-YEAR PR PLAN

A Guide for Advocates

Benjamin Miller

GAIL K. PICCO   CIVIL SECTOR PRESS   TORONTO

The 100 Year PR Plan: A Guide for Advocates

Library and Archives Canada Cataloguing in Publication

Title: The 100 year PR plan : a guide for advocates / Benjamin Miller.
Other titles: One hundred year PR plan
Names: Miller, Benjamin, 1992- author.
Description: Includes bibliographical references.
Identifiers: Canadiana (print) 20200404423 | Canadiana (ebook) 20200404474 |
    ISBN 9781927375662 (softcover) | ISBN 9781927375686 (HTML)
Subjects: LCSH: Nonprofit organizations—Public relations.
Classification: LCC HD62.6 .M55 2021 | DDC 659.2—dc23

Publisher: Civil Sector Press
Canada
Box 86, Station C, Toronto, Ontario, M6J 3M7 Canada
Telephone: 416.267.1287
hilborn-charityenews.ca

United States of America
2626 Glenway Ave, Cincinnati, OH 45204 USA
Telephone: 513.471.6622
Editor: Gail Picco
Book design and production: Cranberryink

To my parents, because care
is the precondition of politics.

Contents

CONTENTS

Acknowledgments

As you will learn in this book, a text is best understood as a response to the author's specific environment. It is therefore crucial both for the author and the reader to know who to thank. And I have no shortage of people to thank.

First and foremost, I must thank my parents who taught me that words should be weighed and not counted, that politics is not a dirty word but a moral imperative, and, to paraphrase Bob Marley, that in this bright future we can't forget our past.

Secondly, I want to thank Rabbi Chaim Boyarsky who taught me if something needs doing the question is never "whether" but only "how" and, to quote Tracy Chapman, "We all must live our lives always feeling always thinking the moment has arrived."

Thirdly, I want to thank Professors Robert Sparling and Paul Saurette. The former, for introducing me to the work of Quentin Skinner as well as providing an incubator for the underlying approach to teaching in this book. The latter, for getting me to think about method more rigorously and for introducing me to the work of James Tully whose approach to Skinner inspired this book.

Fourthly, I want to thank Gail Picco. This simply would not have happened without her openness and immediate ability to spot potential. In fact, if you're ever wondering how precarious every book is, consider that the idea for this was originally one line at the bottom of an email filled with details about something else I was much more excited about but probably wouldn't interest anyone else. Her recommendations have kept this work clearer and focused on you, the reader.

Fifthly, I want to thank my brother Joshua, whose approach to writing keeps me humble, and Tamar, who taught me how inspiring Trees of Heaven and Siberian Elms are.

Sixthly, I want to thank all my test readers, Tali Chernin, Brenda Doner, and Guillaume Lacombe-Kishibe. So much of the nuance is thanks to the depth of their reactions, insight, and suggestions. Their time and willingness to help will be for the benefit of all. I would be remiss if I did not specially thank Guillaume. Every book is a dialogue, and he is always my interlocutor.

Finally, I want to thank the Huron-Wendat, the Seneca, and the Mississaugas of the Credit River on whose traditional lands I wrote this book. I am beginning to learn how to learn from it and it has provided the setting for many walks at crucial times.

There are, of course, many others to whom I am grateful, but the book has to start at some point...

Chapter 1

Let a Thousand Trees of Heaven Grow

"One day Honi was journeying on the road and he saw a man planting a carob tree. He asked, "How long does it take [for this tree] to bear fruit?" The man replied: "Seventy years." Honi then further asked him: "Are you certain that you will live another seventy years?" The man replied: "I found [already grown] carob trees in the world; as my forefathers planted those for me so I too plant these for my children."[1]

You use words every day as you fight for the causes dear to you.

Words are the *terrain* of political life, the field upon which political battles are fought and gardens planted. Words, like physical terrain, shift and change — sometimes slowly over generations, sometimes with shocking suddenness. There are many valuable books about reshaping that terrain in the moment, or even over the next three to five years. This is a book about the kind of changes that may take 100 years.

Why should nonprofits plan their communications 100 years ahead when you can barely guess what is going to happen next week? Like the man who planted the carob tree, it is not because we can live to

---

[1] Babylonian Talmud Tractate Ta'anit 23a.

see their fruit, but because we learn from history that the trees that stand today were results of the efforts of the past. As a nonprofit leader, I am sure that you look out at the world you inhabit and see the concrete and glass of systems that have been built over a living world that struggles to survive beneath. Day after day, you plant seeds and try to tend what grows, but the forest, a different living system, never seems to emerge.

But the concrete is never as solid as it looks. What we take to be foundational today is the unplanned result of struggles of the past.[2] If you walk the streets of downtown Toronto, you will observe Trees of Heaven and Siberian Elms growing and thriving in the slightest cracks disturbing the concrete around them, struggling quite successfully against their inhospitable surroundings. The same is true for our social systems. This book is about how to systematically cultivate those trees and channel their growth until the living forest does indeed emerge.

A BOOK ABOUT MORE THAN TREES

At this point you may be wondering "Is he going to spend the rest of this book talking about trees?" For better or worse, the answer is no. What I will offer you is a step-by-step guide to long-term ideological transformation based on the work of Quentin Skinner as interpreted by James Tully. You will learn how to identify opportunities in existing language, strategize about change, and seize crises when they come until the words you need emerge to make new kinds of justice possible.

Every step of the way, I will use Quentin Skinner's theories to explain why some of the current advice you will find in works on strategic communications and marketing may undermine your ability to create the kind of change you want.

WHO IS *THE 100-YEAR PR PLAN* FOR?

This book is written people who want to take a longer view of their work. In particular, it will provide immediately practical exercises to

---

[2] James Tully, ed., "The pen is a mightier sword: Quentin Skinner's analysis of politics," in *Meaning & Context: Quentin Skinner and his Critics*, ed. James Tully (Princeton: Princeton University Press, 1988), 19.

leaders of nonprofit organizations as well as those responsible for nonprofit communications who want to think beyond the typical three to five years strategic plan. You don't need to have a specific job title or any specific training. You just need to have an interest in how best to help set the strategic direction of your organization or how the organization communicates to achieve its goals. If you are an individual looking to make a systemic impact, but not currently associated with an organization, this book will nevertheless be useful to you.

You could work full-time at a large nonprofit corporation or volunteer at a grassroots association in any sector. I will give examples throughout the book that speak to diverse sectors, movements, types of organizations, and sometimes just individuals. It's not so much who you are but what it is you want to say that makes this book right for you. The plan laid out in this book is specifically designed for people working towards systemic change or for organizations who need ideological transformation before they can accomplish their goals.

What is "Ideological Transformation"?

The word "ideology" has many meanings and is a heavily contested concept. For our purposes though, when I use the word, I mean "a language of politics" that is used to discuss the issues that you are interested in.[3] By "language", I don't just mean vocabulary, although I will sometimes use the term "moral vocabulary" to describe this. By "ideology", "language of politics" and "moral vocabulary", I mean the words, symbols, and rules that govern how we convince people to support or oppose things. We are going to be most interested in the language used by those who exercise control over the issues you care about. They could be businesses, government offices, civil society organizations, or individuals. What that language is will govern whether your issue is considered acceptable or problematic and what solutions are considered legitimate or illegitimate for those institutions or individuals.

You may not use the term "ideological transformation" to describe your goals, but if you think the *way* people think is an obstacle to

---

[3] Tully, ed., *Meaning & Context,* 9.

changing the world, then you are probably seeking ideological trans-formation at some level. Many, if not most, organizations probably want to change the way people think to some degree, if only to get those people to prioritize donating to them.

The 100-Year PR Plan is for you if your goal seems so far away from the current mainstream thinking (or action) on the topic that it seems like at the current pace it could take 100 years to get to where you want to go. It may be that what you think is a major issue, other people don't even see as a problem. Or perhaps what you think should be acceptable, other people find highly problematic. It could be that people agree with you that something is or is not a problem but think your way of approaching it is too extreme for one reason or another. In some of the most frustrating situations, it could be that everyone says they agree with you, but their actions tell a very different story.

If this sounds like your situation, then you may have noticed the deck is stacked against you when it comes to the language people use to talk about the problem or the solution you are proposing. *The 100-Year PR Plan* is to help you get the language in which an issue or solution is described on your side. As you probably know, language is just one of many barriers you might face. It's also only one of many resources that you'll need to achieve your mission. *The 100-Year PR Plan* will not on its own overcome the other barriers or provide you with those other resources, although it can help.

WHAT THIS BOOK IS AND IS NOT AND HOW TO GET THE MOST OUT OF IT

It's no good to promise someone the moon and only give them a cow. But cows are great, and many people will be pleased if provided with one. I therefore want to make clear from the beginning that I am not a communications expert and it would be claiming too much to call this book's method "surefire". Rather, it offers you a framework to think more deeply. It will help you learn more from the examples of history and think more systematically about how you communicate. More than a method, I hope this book cultivates how you think and feel about strategic communications. Ultimately, therefore, whether you choose to integrate the whole method into your practices, some of the exercise, or just start to see communications in a more disciplined way, you will gain something from this book.

What This Book is Not: A Surefire Method Based on Decades of My Own Experience

Before going any further, though, I should confess a few things. Books on nonprofit communications are usually written by communications professionals with years of experience in communications roles in the nonprofit sector. I am not a communications professional with years of experience in the nonprofit sector. I have not practiced this method at several successful organizations that I can name for you, nor can I provide pictures illustrating the fruits of my labour. Why then should you spend your limited time reading this book?

As I mentioned, this book is based on the theories of Quentin Skinner. He is a historian who has studied hundreds of years of writings by various kinds of political actors that changed the world in enormous ways. He has meticulously documented the strategies they consciously and unconsciously used to foster that societal transformation. Even if I had decades of experience in the sector, it would pale in comparison to the hundreds of years in accumulated wisdom that Skinner's methods attempt to capture.

It's not so much that his theories are uncontested truths, but his methods offer a systematic window into the overwhelming hodge-podge of historical facts that have so much to offer us. In long-term complex societal change, I would be skeptical of anyone offering a surefire way to succeed. Rather, by sticking to one interesting vantage point, Skinner's, we have a disciplined way to notice certain assumptions in the current advice and take away lessons from the treasure trove of history. My hope is that you will see the proof is in the pudding of the pages that follow. And who doesn't like pudding?[4]

What This Book is: A Conversation Between History and Nonprofit Communications Advice

Skinner was trying to understand the past, not provide a book of tactics for people trying to change the future. And he certainly was not speaking to the specific context of nonprofit organizations. I tried

---

[4] OK, probably a lot of people. The book isn't for everyone.

to make his theories relevant to you in two ways. Firstly, I tried to put him in conversation with current nonprofit communications writing. Secondly, I tried to provide contemporary and historical examples of nonprofits and social movements practicing techniques that are precisely what Skinner describes.

The conversation from the perspective of nonprofit communication advice is based on an extensive search of books and articles mainly about strategic communications, a search that might replicate the one that a diligent nonprofit leader without specialized training in communications would do. But the research is extensive enough to show broader patterns and commonalities in the kind of advice nonprofits are receiving.

I chose this method for a few reasons. I wanted to draw on and understand existing practices in the nonprofit sector (mainly in North America). I did not feel a need to do an exhaustive review of communications literature because my goal in writing this book is not to critique the most cutting-edge advice communications specialists have to offer, but rather engage with the kind of advice those without access to the cutting-edge might receive through a limited search online and visiting their library.

It should be clear from what I've said above that *The 100-Year PR Plan* is a hypothesis rather than a tried-and-true method. Because I cannot vouch for this method based on its past results, and I don't have the ability to offer you a money-back guarantee, I will instead point to the special and systematic vantage point Skinner offers you on how you communicate with the world. Even though *The 100-Year PR Plan* is a step-by-step method which you can systematically implement, it is also a frame of mind for thinking about political communications. To use a cooking metaphor, my main goal is not so much to offer you a recipe book so much as to cultivate your taste.

This approach was also taken by one of history's most infamous writers of advice books, Niccolò Machiavelli.[5] While it is helpful to have a recipe to follow, becoming a good cook is much more a matter

---

[5] Niccolo Machiavelli, *The Discourses* (New York: Penguin Books, 2003), 98.

of practice than it is about coming up with rules.[6] The trouble is, you don't have an extra 100 years to do a test run.

According to Machiavelli, the best replacement is to serve as an "apprentice" to the great examples of history. As I mentioned above, I tried to make Skinner relevant to the nonprofit sector context by drawing on a wide range of examples from across movements, sectors, organization types, countries, and ages. In doing so, I also hope to provide you with the kind of apprenticeship long-term societal transformation requires according to Machiavelli.

How to Get the Most Out of it: Summary, Sensibility, and Method

Most chapters in this book are dedicated to an important topic in nonprofit communications. There are three parts to each chapter:

1. A summary of conventional advice on that topic.

2. How, according to Skinner's theories, this advice may limit your ability to engage in ideologically transformative communications.

3. How you can put Skinner's theories into practice in a way that overcomes these limitations.

And there are three ways you can read this book.

1. If you are new to nonprofit communications, reading the first part of each chapter will give you a solid introduction to current practices and thinking. Even if you are not new, it can be a helpful reference and cites many useful resources.

2. If you are familiar with the current practices and thinking in nonprofit communications, then reading the second part of each chapter should help deepen and sharpen your perspective on communications. It may help you to understand the broader historical significance of developments in your sector or why certain practices keep failing.

3. If you want to systematically implement your own 100-Year PR Plan, then the third part of each chapter will provide you with the steps, tools, and exercises to do so.

---

[6] Michael Oakeshott, *Rationalism in politics and other essays*, (Indianapolis: Liberty Fund, 1991), 16-17.

Ultimately, I believe you will have the most satisfying experience by reading the whole book straight through. Each part of each chapter builds on and responds to the one before it. In the first part, I situate you in the current thinking. In the second part, I show you the limits. In the third part, I show you how to overcome these limits.

Without further ado, let the next 100 years of your life begin!

Chapter 2

Skinner and His Method

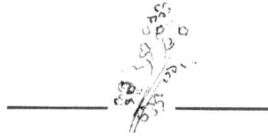

_____ * _____

Before we jump into discussing specific topics in strategic communications, it will be helpful for you to understand a bit about the intellectual context of Skinner's career, what his method is, and why it's such a useful framework for your communications. This chapter will give you the foundation you need to understand the coming chapters and the word map you will need for all the coming exercises.

More specifically, you will learn:

- What an **innovating ideologist** is and does
- What a **keyword** in a moral vocabulary is
- How keywords include a **sense, reference,** and **judgment value**
- How to build **a word map** that shows the way words relate to one another.

SKINNER'S CONTEXT: READ OUTSIDE THE BOX

Quentin Skinner entered the study of history in the 60s at the University of Cambridge in order to become a teacher.[7] Owing to a

---

[7] Anonymous Project Officer, "Making History: The Changing Face of the Profession in Britain", interview with Quentin Skinner, April 18, 2008.

change in British higher education policy, there was suddenly a large demand for teachers, and he got that chance.

Having only just completed his bachelor's degree at Cambridge, he was appointed as a Fellow at Christ's College and began teaching immediately.[8] Since then, over the past 40 years, Quentin Skinner has become a respected historian known for his work on the methods of historical research, the political theories of Niccolò Machiavelli and Thomas Hobbes, and the interplay of political thought and action during the European Renaissance and Reformation.

Only 37 years old at the time, Skinner was elected to the position of Professor of Political Science at the University of Cambridge in 1978,[9] a significant accomplishment that recognized the huge impact he had already made through many books and articles, including *The Foundations of Modern Political Thought*. Designated by the Time Literary Supplement as one of the 100 most influential books since World War II, *The Foundations of Modern Political Thought* is a three-volume *magnum opus*.

Why was it so ground-breaking? As Skinner himself explains it, there were two "orthodox" ways of approaching classic works of political theory when he started his studies.[10] The first was to find the meaning of a text by situating it in the context of "religious, political, and economic factors" of the time it was written. For example, Marxist scholars viewed texts as merely products of the underlying class struggle of the time. The second, more widely accepted approach, was to treat the text as autonomous from its surroundings, something that can be understood on its own. For example, students of Leo Strauss viewed the great works as participating in age-old debates about universal questions. The first approach reduced works of political theory to little more than artifacts of their times. The second approach put texts into timeless conversations with one another, almost totally ignoring the actual environment in which they were written.

Influenced by a small dissenting school of historians before him, Skinner's method chose a third path. Fundamentally, he understood

---

[8] Encyclopedia Britannica. Quentin Skinner in Encyclopedia Britannica, 2019.

[9] Tully, ed., *Meaning & Context*, 3.

[10] Tully, ed., *Meaning & Context*, 29-67.

texts as political acts of the author, intervening in pressing conversations that were happening at the time of writing. For example, think of how X-Men spoke to the civil rights movements going on at the time. The authors are neither the mere passive product of their environment nor mere theorists participating in a timeless debate about ideas. Rather, they are human beings with pressing needs and political agency. According to one historian, the "Skinnerian revolution" consisted not so much in its methodology but in its restoring of the idea of political activity and, specifically, writing as a form of political activity.[11] This was quite novel. By understanding authors as political agents, we come to better appreciate the impact our own communications can have.

SKINNER'S METHOD: YOUR SPEECH SHIFTS THE SANDS BENEATH YOUR FEET

Writing, and communicating more broadly, contributes something very important to political conflicts. By changing the words or text around an issue, our communications have the power to change the structure of how people think and therefore what they will accept or push back against. In this book, I call that process "ideological change". To understand Skinner's method is to understand how he thinks people accomplish those changes.

Innovating Ideologists Make Ideological Changes

Skinner calls the people who bring about these ideological changes, "innovating ideologists".[12] These authors respond to the political problems of their times, either because they want to address their own desires, (e.g., get into public office), or the public's, (e.g., liberate them from tyrannical regimes).[13] Innovating ideologists are people who want to do something, want others to do something, or who are already doing something that is questioned by the broader society. For example, Skinner discusses the example of 17th century merchants who were accumulating large amounts of wealth, which

---

[11] Encyclopedia Britannica. Quentin Skinner in Encyclopedia Britannica, 2019.

[12] Skinner, Quentin, *Visions of Politics* (Cambridge: Cambridge University Press, 2002), 145–57.

[13] Tully, ed., *Meaning & Context*, 10.

was looked down upon in the religious society of the time.[14] They needed to make ideological changes so that their activities could be accepted.

This is essentially the equivalent to what in our times is called the "social license to operate" which describes acceptance by the public of undertaking certain business activities.[15] A person can keep doing something even without social license, or with only partial social license. However, when you operate without complete social license it will come at an increased cost such as protests, delays, and legal challenges.[16]

For example, companies may ultimately be able to build a pipeline across the territory of the Wet'suwet'en. However, it will not have been without an additional cost to shareholders caused by the political and legal questions it raised in the minds of many individuals and institutions. Alternatively, nonprofits can operate safe injection sites, but it will not be without additional delays and uncertainties that other programs geared towards overdose prevention do not face. Both face issues of legitimacy to make their operations work. Both may fail if they cannot overcome this legitimacy issue or proceed by force.

Innovating ideologists may also want to make something that is currently acceptable unacceptable.[17] It is not hard to think of examples in this category. Environmentalists protesting the oil sands. Feminists attempting to end violence against women. Vegans attempting to end the consumption of animals and animal by-products.

A more subtle example is the Decent Work movement in the nonprofit sector which aims to improve working conditions for workers in the nonprofit sector. They use a mix of tactics including making previously acceptable activities unacceptable (e.g., ending low wages) and making previously unacceptable activities acceptable (e.g., more funding for administrative costs).[18]

---

[14] Skinner, *Visions of Politics*, 147-57.
[15] "What is the Social License?" https://socialicense.com/definition.html.
[16] Skinner, *Visions of Politics*, 156.
[17] Skinner, *Visions of Politics*, 149.
[18] Ontario Nonprofit Network, "Decent Work".

Ideological Change is Filling a Justification Gap

You may want to make something unacceptable acceptable or the reverse. My point is that Skinner highlights how ideological innovation begins with a justification gap of some kind. A justification gap is a gap between what you think should be acceptable and what actually is accepted. The next crucial step is to understand where a justification gap comes from.

A justification gap occurs when you are not able to marshal the existing moral language of your audience to legitimize the desired course of action.[19] Language plays a very important role in legitimizing actions, especially of those in power.[20] It does not matter if a person believes the justifications they offer, although it is often important for a person's self-image that they believe what they are doing is legitimate on some level. But even if they do not believe what they say at all, it is all about the ability of language to help them in overcoming opposition and in moving others, as we discussed above.

To begin with, therefore, you only have the existing moral vocabulary of your audience to work with. By moral vocabulary, I mean the keywords in language that both judge and describe a thing at the same time.[21] For example, "cheap" both describes the price of something and judges its quality or value. What moral vocabulary you are dealing with is a question about the prevalent morality of the society, or relevant part of society you are trying to persuade.[22] So the justification gap emerges when you are unable, using the current common understanding of those words,[23] to get your point across.

Filling a Justification Gap Means Using Keywords in Novel Ways

When innovating ideologists use language to fill a justification gap, they don't just do it by saying "hey we need to fill this gap!". Rather,

---

[19] Skinner, *Visions of Politics*, 147.

[20] Skinner, *Visions of Politics*, 173.

[21] Skinner, *Visions of Politics*, 160 – 162.

[22] Skinner, *Visions of Politics*, 156.

[23] Skinner is careful to point out that how words are understood is are always contested so that it is never more than an ideological posture to claim that a particular understanding of a word is standard. I use the term "prevalent", therefore, as a more neutral expression denoting that the word is more likely to be understood a particular way. See Skinner, *Visions of Politics*, 182.

Skinner's point is that, consciously or not, the way innovating ideologists use moral keywords to communicate their message itself tries to fill the gap. They do this by using the keywords in a way that is new to the audience and so changes how the audience understands those words.[24] I could say "smoking causes fatalities." or I could say "How is your death stick?" Both may communicate the same message, but the latter builds it into the language.

To take a more in-depth look, let us briefly examine the Vegan Society of Canada's website.

CASE 1: VEGAN SOCIETY OF CANADA

Vegan philosophy and lifestyle

We are a registered non-profit corporation. Our mission can be explained in many pages or a few words: Reduce harm for the benefit of humans, animals and the environment. Our main way to achieve this is to promote the adoption of a vegan lifestyle.

The promotion of a vegan lifestyle achieves our dual charitable purpose of protecting and maintaining both the public's health and the environment. We do this through various means like public outreach, articles, information sessions, etc. As a member of the Vegan World Alliance (VWA) we adhere to the shared vision and mission of the VWA.

Unfortunately, so much funding goes towards small companion animals often because even though donors would like to help all animals, there is no Canada wide charitable organization to do so. Please join us in our efforts to benefits all animals, including human animals, and the environment through a vegan lifestyle.

Legal workshop

We aim to develop legal workshops so that people across the country can safely exercise their right to demonstrate peacefully and intervene or disrupt when the law permits. Contact us for more details or to help make this a reality.

Keywords on the Vegan Society of Canada website homepage include harm, benefit, human, animal, environment, vegan lifestyle, vegan philosophy, charitable, public health, human animals, community, demonstrate peacefully, intervene, and disrupt.[25]

It is not enough to just look up the dictionary definitions of these words (though that may be helpful). According to Skinner, if you want

---

[24] Skinner, *Visions of Politics*, 133.
[25] Vegan Society of Canada, *Vegan Philosophy and Lifestyle* (May 18, 2020).

to understand a keyword you need to ask yourself "What can I *do* with it?". You must appreciate how a keyword can be used in an argument to advance or oppose broader social philosophies.[26] There are three aspects to every word that a nonprofit facing a justification gap may want to take issue with and therefore understand.[27]

1. **The "sense" of the word**. This is typically what we think of when we think of a word's meaning or definition.

2. **The "reference" of a word**. This is the range of situations in which it is considered appropriate to use that word.

3. **The "judgment value" of the word.** This is the standard range of attitudes the word can be used to express.

In the figure below, I have loosely sketched a brief outline of what I take to be the common sense, reference, and attitudes associated with some of the keywords identified on the Vegan Society of Canada website. Obviously, this is a contentious exercise. I do not suppose my initial impressions of these words to be authoritative but rather to illustrate the kind of detail one should consider. In practice, if you wanted to analyze a website like this, you should be or work with someone much more familiar with the history and context of veganism.

- **"Harm"**: it is not the *sense* but the *reference* that might give rise to a debate between a vegan and a non-vegan. Both might agree "harm" means something being hurt or deprived of something they need in a morally unacceptable way but disagree whether a case of an animal being slaughtered for food is a case this keyword should apply to.

- **"Animal"**: the very use of the term "human animal" later on the page reinforces the Vegan Society's efforts to situate humans as just one of many animals as opposed to separately from the general class of animals. What is important to note is that even if someone agrees to the technical definition of "animal", they may still be uncomfortable with the use of the word "human animal" in this way (indeed I once had just such a conversation with someone who was vehemently opposed

---

[26] Skinner, *Visions of Politics*, 176.
[27] Skinner, *Visions of Politics*, 161-162.

to its use). This shows us that ideological innovation is not just about the words but the relationship between them.

- **"Peaceful demonstration"**: a vegan and non-vegan may agree about the *reference* and the *attitude* we should have towards peaceful demonstration but disagree about what is included in the term (i.e., its *sense*). In this case, the Vegan Society includes activities that may be called "disruptions". For some, calling a disruption a peaceful demonstration might be a contradiction in terms. On the other hand, by definition, a disruption will be more likely to call attention to itself. The result is that an argument over the legitimate bounds of "peaceful" or "disruption" may really be a disagreement over what tools different people think should be available for a given cause.

The sense, reference, and attitude of some vegan society of Canada keywords

Word	Senses	Reference	Attitude
Harm	Physical injury or mental damage.[28]	Usually applies when we consider the thing experiencing the sense of harm to be normatively valuable and capable of feeling. For example, you may not say "you harmed that dandelion" unless you particularly cared about dandelions.	It is a bad thing that should be avoided. If there is no justification for it, it is generally viewed as morally right to minimize and eliminate it if possible.
Animal	Any member of the kingdom Animalia, comprising multicellular organisms that have a well-defined shape and usually limited growth, can move voluntarily, actively acquire food and digest it internally, and have sensory and nervous systems that allow them to respond rapidly to stimuli: some classification schemes also include protozoa and certain other single-celled eukaryotes that have mobility and animal-like nutritional modes.	Usually does not refer to humans. May refer to all animals except humans.	Sometimes neutral. May be used in a pejorative sense to express ferocity, e.g., "the attacker was an animal", or to express the carnal nature of human beings, as in the song "Bad Touch" by Bloodhound Gang. Sometimes deeply negative. For example, when groups of people are likened to or called the names of different animals as a strategy to dehumanize them.
Peaceful demonstration	An expression of dissent or dissatisfaction without the use of violence.	Usually is conflated with protests that respect the law.[29] Some may deny this label to any expression of a view they disagree with as "disruptive" though will likely not admit this is what they are doing.	Positive expression of democratic rights and civic mindedness. Attempts to suppress this form of activity are therefore open to powerful condemnation of authoritarian, tyrannical, or otherwise anti-democratic purpose.

---

[28] Dictionary.com "harm" https://www.dictionary.com/browse/harm?s=t.

[29] Cambridge Dictionary, "peaceful protest" https://dictionary.cambridge.org/example/english/peaceful-protest.

Using Keywords in a Novel Way Means Insisting on Their Current Meaning

There are three points here. Firstly, I hope this brief exercise shows that even a short text on your website can often implicitly advance a number of complex and contentious ideological arguments. These texts implicitly make these arguments by using the words in the way they want people to understand them.

Secondly, this shows how the extent of agreement over the sense, reference, and judgment in keywords varies depending on who is speaking. However, there must be some basic agreement for meaningful disagreement to be possible. Indeed, if there wasn't a certain basic agreement between conflicting parties, there wouldn't really be an argument so much as two parties talking past each other.[30] In order to convince someone of an innovation, it is necessary to show how the proposed innovation is in fact "truer" to some other aspect of the word's meaning that both parties agree on. For example, the vegan might insist on a very conservative adherence to the technical definition of animal in order to advance what might be a very innovative understanding of how the word "human" relates to it.

This is, I think, one of Skinner's most crucial and interesting points. The more radical an organization is, the more it will have to seek support in the existing moral vocabulary. So, for example, rather than claim they were doing something totally new, leaders of the Christian Reformation insisted they were returning to the original spirit of Christianity and it was the existing authorities who had departed from that original spirit.[31] This leads Skinner to say that every revolutionary is to this extent forced to march into battle backwards.[32]

Seeing the Moral Vocabularies You Need to Change Holistically

Thirdly, I hope the above exercise shows how words should not be viewed in isolation but in terms of their relationship to one another. Skinner emphasizes that moral vocabularies are holistic so that when we scan the existing state of the field to see what we have to work

---

[30] Skinner, *Visions of Politics*, 165.

[31] Skinner, Quentin, *The Foundations of Modern Political Thought Volume 2: The Age of Reformation* (Cambridge: Cambridge University Press 2004), 27.

[32] Skinner, *Visions of Politics*, 149-150.

with "we must be prepared to focus not on the 'normal structure' of particular words, but rather on their role in upholding complete social philosophies."[33]

We cannot understand "animal" in a vacuum but must understand its connection to the term "human". In turn, we cannot understand "human" without understanding certain keywords that have been used to set humans apart, such as "speech", "consciousness", "reason", "free will", "feeling", etc. The more you ripple outwards in identifying keywords and their relationship to each other, the better sense of your present context you will have. Not only that, but to understand these words you will have to learn about their history.

Identifying as much of the total structure of relevant words as possible is important for at least two reasons. It will alert you to potentially unintended consequences your strategies may have, as well as unexpected allies you may be able to recruit.[34] And, it will help you understand why some words are so difficult and others are much easier to change. Changing moral vocabularies is like playing a game of Jenga. It is much harder to take a brick from certain parts of the tower because the weight of the other bricks rest on it.

For example, who is considered a "person" has enormous implications throughout the law and public policy. It is entrenched in various official ways. Communicators must be sensitive to the various ways in which words are institutionally entrenched because those entrenchments will raise the stakes of a keyword's meaning and pose resistance to any obvious efforts to change it.

For example, if animals were recognized as persons and thus having the rights of persons, it would entail a huge transformation of society. A lot of other bricks rest on the relationship of "animal" to "person". The *size* of the implication alone, without asking whether it would be a good or bad development, is likely to provoke significant resistance on its own. "Harm", on the other hand, is a more fluid term which is difficult to define and more contentious philosophically. It is a looser brick and riper for dispute.

---

[33] Skinner, *Visions of Politics*, 165.
[34] Skinner, *Visions of Politics*, 164.

Moral Vocabularies Enable but Also Constrain

It is important to recognize that ideological change geared towards enabling new action will always also have a constraining effect on the one who adopts that position.[35] Once you have claimed justification in terms of a particular moral vocabulary, you are then constrained in your ability to do things which run counter to that vocabulary, due to the risk of appearing disingenuous or hypocritical.

It will also, in this way, direct a decision-maker's attention to actions which are more coherently justified by the range of their commitments than others.[36] For instance, a politician that calls themselves a feminist will likely be held to a higher standard on certain issues than one that has never adopted the term. This can be a powerful tool for constraining other actors who have adopted a certain kind of justification.

THE PROBLEM: HOW SKINNER CAN HELP THE NONPROFIT SECTOR

There are many fascinating explanations of how ideological change happens. Why should you use Skinner's approach to structure your strategic communications?

What makes his work so useful to you is that he explains how some of the most transformative works in history were written as specific answers to pressing political questions of their time. They were never just works of theory, but tools that the authors created for broader movements, to build on momentum, seize moments, and chart a new course for their societies and ultimately the world. Skinner analyzes these texts in terms of the specific writing techniques the authors used to transform the meaning of the words they were using. I want to make these tools available to you. You don't need a big budget, just a quill, pen, typewriter, or computer will do.

Ideological change is going on all around us. Every time you try to convince people to see the world in a genuinely new light, you are already trying to bring about ideological change. On one level, therefore, Skinner is just describing what he sees happening. On the other hand, as Skinner points out, just because this is what people do does not mean

---

[35] Skinner, *Visions of Politics*, 155.

[36] Skinner, *Visions of Politics*, 174.

they do it well.[37] The point of this book's method is to make you aware of one system of thought about how ideological change happens so you can spend your limited resources in a more systematic and targeted way.

Commentators on Skinner have called this the "rhetorical perspective".[38] I do not claim this is the only book you will ever need nor the only book that will be helpful to you. It is one technique that, if I faithfully applied Skinner's thinking and he has truly captured historical events, has been useful in effecting large scale change in the past. I think it lends itself well to a step-by-step process and for that reason gives you a systematic way to pursue your long-term goals in your communications.

THE SOLUTION: BUILD YOUR WORD MAP

In order to make a strategy, you first have to map out the terrain, i.e., the existing common moral vocabulary you are working with. That means identifying your keywords, describing their sense, reference, and judgment value, and visualizing how they relate to one another.

1. Gather Keywords

The first step is for you, or a designated researcher on your team, to gather the keywords that make up the common moral vocabulary you are working with. Start by thinking about whose mind you want to change and what they read, watch, or listen to.

Sources discussing your issue you might want to look at include:

- Conventional books (i.e., book where you think to yourself "I've seen this all before.")
- Classic books (i.e., books people often reference or quote)
- News and magazine articles
- Government, think tank, and NGO reports
- Blogs
- Websites of organizations working on issue (particularly home page and about us)

---

[37] Skinner, *Visions of Politics*, 150.
[38] Skinner, *Visions of Politics*, 179.

- Promotional materials like brochures, tweets, and other social media posts
- Popular radio and podcasts
- Events and panels
- Documentaries or films on the issue
- Popular songs about the issue (whether the message is explicit or not)
- Comics (whether the message is explicit or not)

Go through each source looking for keywords (or phrases). Remember keywords are those that simultaneously describe and judge what they are describing. A good test is to ask yourself "how does this word make me feel?". If the answer is "nothing", it's probably not a keyword. For example, if your issue was the promotion of social finance, "entrepreneur" and "employment" may be included but "implement" may not be, even though it is used a lot. You only need to record each keyword once, although it can be helpful to take note of how often the author uses a particular word.

As you can see, there are many potential sources. You do not have to go through everything. A good time to stop is when you reach a saturation point and see the same words over and over again. If you do not have the time or resources to carry out a thorough search, do not fret. Simply talking to a few people who have been involved in the issue, and reading a few key reports, websites, and social media posts should give you a sense of the common lingo. If you have 5 sources from fairly diverse mediums and places, you are in good shape.

Record each source and word in a spreadsheet like the example below. It's important to include the reference so that if the person doing the research has to leave, others can easily pick it back up.

Spreadsheet #1: Identifying keywords

	A	B	C
1	Source	Keyword	Reference
2	Vegan Society of Canada Home Page	Harm	Vegan Society of Canada (May 18, 2020), Vegan Philosophy and Lifestyle Available at: https://www.vegancanada.org/
3	Vegan Society of Canada Home Page	benefit	Vegan Society of Canada (May 18, 2020), Vegan Philosophy and Lifestyle Available at: https://www.vegancanada.org/
4	Vegan Society of Canada Home Page	human	Vegan Society of Canada (May 18, 2020), Vegan Philosophy and Lifestyle Available at: https://www.vegancanada.org/
5	Vegan Society of Canada Home Page	animal	Vegan Society of Canada (May 18, 2020), Vegan Philosophy and Lifestyle Available at: https://www.vegancanada.org/
6	Vegan Society of Canada Home Page	human animal	Vegan Society of Canada (May 18, 2020), Vegan Philosophy and Lifestyle Available at: https://www.vegancanada.org/
7	Vegan Society of Canada Home Page	environment	Vegan Society of Canada (May 18, 2020), Vegan Philosophy and Lifestyle Available at: https://www.vegancanada.org/

2. Identify Conventional Sense, Reference, and Judgment Value

Once you have identified keywords, you will want to determine how the author is using these words, i.e., the sense, reference, and judgments they are using the word to convey. This part of the exercise really relies on your judgment. It can help to have someone else working with you or a team of two researchers who have different enough perspectives to keep each other in check. Ultimately, your analysis will be limited by your understanding, but it is still helpful to go through the exercise of parsing out the sense, reference, and judgment.

For each keyword, ask yourself:

1. **Sense:** What is the definition of this word the way they are using it? (bonus points if they actually define it!)
2. **Reference:** What is the situation they have applied it in?
3. **Judgment:** What is the author trying to make me feel by using this word?

Record the sense, reference, and judgment by creating three more columns in your spreadsheet.

Spreadsheet #2: Identify sense, reference and judgment

Source	Keyword	Sense	Reference	Judgment	Reference
Vegan Society of Canada Home Page	Harm	hurt? Vague	applies to humans, animals, and environments	Bad. We should stop it.	Vegan Society of Canada (May 18, 2(Lifestyle Available at: https://www.
Vegan Society of Canada Home Page	benefit	vague.	humans, animals, and environments are capable of being benefited	Good. We should support it.	Vegan Society of Canada (May 18, 2(Lifestyle Available at: https://www.
Vegan Society of Canada Home Page	human	species. Homo sapiens. One of many types of animals	Usual.	Not singularly important apart from other animals.	Vegan Society of Canada (May 18, 2(Lifestyle Available at: https://www.

Once you have reviewed a number of sources, sort your spreadsheet by keyword instead of source. This will immediately tell you a few things. It will tell you which words are used more frequently. You will also be able to see the sense, reference, and judgment side-by-side and start to compare.

You may see all the sense, reference, and judgment being very similar to one another. This will be a very settled word.

You may see a few sub-groupings or consistency in parts of the word (e.g., sense), but not others (e.g., reference). This will tell you the word either has multiple meanings or is undergoing a well-defined contest.

You may be dealing with language that is so contested that there are no two authors who use it the same way. In that case, focus on the conventional meaning for your specific audience and prioritize that. If there is still no conventional meaning it either means the word is ripe for seizing and being given a definite meaning, or it is so confused and contested you should avoid it, as it will lead to much distraction. We'll talk about this more in a later chapter.

Ultimately, you should write a report with a table for each word summarizing (as I did in the last section) what you see as the conventional sense, reference, and judgment, as well as noting where and how this is contested.

3. Connect Your Keywords to each Other and Other Keywords

Once you have completed Step 2, you can identify the words that your keywords depend on. Look at what words you or the author chose to define your keywords. Do a quick search for each word online and repeat the exercise of identifying the sense, reference, and judgment of each keyword as it is used in these sources. Try to limit yourself to sources that are most closely connected to your time, place, and audience. You can repeat this process as many times as you'd like to get as wide a picture of how your keywords fit into broader moral languages as possible. In your spreadsheet, try to separate each layer of analysis so you know which are your "core keywords" and which are one degree or more removed.

Now you should start to connect your keywords. This can be done on PowerPoint or similar software. If you prefer, you can also get out some good old fashioned flip chart paper. I recommend not writing the words directly on the page, since you will probably need to re-arrange them as a structure emerges. Instead, write them on sticky notes and put the sticky notes on the paper.

Put your core keywords in the centre and the words they depend on in a circle on the outside (with more circles for every layer you repeated the exercise).

Draw lines and arrows between your keywords to show how they connect to each other. For example, if two words are presented as opposites by the author (e.g., free speech and political correctness) then draw a red line with an "x" between them.

Draw arrows from the words you used to define other words.

You can also visualize the settled words and contested words by writing each in different colours.

Like a network visualization, this will help you see which words are super connectors in the moral vocabulary (e.g., a lot of words depend on them for their definition). It will also tell you which parts of the vocabulary are settled, and which parts are looser. Being able to do this will be very important in later chapters.

I won't pretend this is a scientific process. Two informed people may come to define the words differently and see different structures. The important thing is that you develop a structure, to improve your ability to see the forest for the trees.

Chapter 3

The Most Important Goal You've Probably Never Set

"Where does a thought go when it's forgotten?"

—Sigmund Freud

When it comes to setting strategic communications goals, the ideological goals you don't set influence your ability to accomplish the goals you do set. In this chapter, we will look at current practices in strategic communications goal setting, why setting ideological change goals is so important, and where to begin the process of setting the right ideological change goals.

More specifically, you will learn:

- Some conventional wisdom on communications goal setting
- How your funding, reputational, and human resources objectives are affected by ideology
- That awareness raising is never just about awareness

- What happens when ideological goals backfire
- How to articulate your mission in a way that highlights the limits of current language.

CONVENTIONAL WISDOM: IT IS IMPORTANT TO SET GOALS

The accepted wisdom in strategic communications planning is that you should begin by setting goals.[39] This process is best done once every 3-5 years in which you articulate a vision for your organization in the near future.[40] Goals are, simply put, what your organization wants.[41] They should answer the questions of what change you want to happen, what will it take to make it happen, and who you will serve by making it happen.[42] Goals can be broken down in several ways:

- **operational**, affecting how you deliver your message (e.g., create an Instagram account),
- **reputational**, affecting how your organization is perceived, or
- **behavioural**, affecting how your employees and volunteers act.[43]

Another way to break down the goals is:

- branding and overall messaging,
- awareness raising,
- increasing size of audience engagement, and
- increasing fundraising.[44]

Another way to think about your communications goals is to think about what key messages you want to get across to the public recorded in concise and jargon-free language.[45] You want these statements to

---

[39] Patterson, S.J., Radtke, J.M. *Strategic Communications for Nonprofit Organizations: Seven Steps to Creating a Successful Plan: Second Edition* (Hoboken, N.J: John Wiley & Sons, 2002), 3.

[40] Patterson and Radtke, 25.

[41] Patterson and Radtke, 25.

[42] Patterson and Radtke, 26.

[43] Kinzey, Ruth Ellen, *Promoting nonprofit organizations: a reputation management approach* (New York: Routledge, 2013), 36.

[44] Queens University of Charlotte, "Best Nonprofit Communication Strategies," 2020.

[45] Kinzey, 36.

be action-oriented and mission-driven. You also want these state-ments to clearly connect your nonprofit's actions, stances, and requests to what your organization is fundamentally about.[46] For example, a health organization fundraising with unhealthy food could send mixed messages.

When the nonprofit sets its goals, it needs to be realistic given the nonprofit's local and global context. Peter C. Brinckerhoff, a nonprofit marketing consultant with decades of experience, suggests a striking metaphor that portrays you as just one small actor in a gigantic context that naturally limits what you can and should say:

> *"Throughout the nonprofit community, the tide has been changing for the past decade. And, like tides, the changes are barely noticeable at first, and are more evident on some parts of the shoreline than others. But once the tide changes, the momentum is reversed, and the outcome is irreversible. The forces at play are too big, too powerful, too global to resist."* [47]

In the books and articles that I consulted, advisors rarely talk about how ideological systems and changes affect the goals you set. Some strategic communications scholars, however, do talk about ideological change. For example, David Ongenaert, a doctoral student at Ghent University Center for Persuasive Communication, discusses how broader ideological debates affect the way refugee-serving nonprofits communicate with the public.[48] Even among nonprofit communi-cations scholars, these discussions are relatively rare.[49] But many scholars and advisors do recognize that the way nonprofits communi-cate to the public can transform society. Nonprofit communications "create awareness around international social, political, economic and environmental issues, expresses particular world visions, shapes collective identities and affects corporate practices and government

---

[46] Kinzey, 36.

[47] Brinckerhoff, Peter C., *Mission-based marketing: positioning your not-for-profit in an increasingly competitive world 3rd ed.*, (Hoboken, NJ: John Wiley & Sons, 2010), 3-4.

[48] Ongenaert, David, "Refugee Organizations' Public Communication: Conceptual-izing and Exploring New Avenues for an Underdeveloped Research Subject," *Media and Communication* 7 No. 2 (2019): 195–206.

[49] Ongenaert, 198.

policies".[50] Similarly, Sally Patterson and Janel Radtke, authors of a well-known strategic communications method, write that strategic communication is key to social change, since every time we communicate about a serious issue we are changed by the process.[51]

Obviously, people intuitively understand that some organizations may force people to ask tough questions about how they think. For example, Kairos, a faith-based human rights organization, has a "Blanket Exercise" which is an immersive experience summarizing the history of Indigenous-settler relations in Canada. The Blanket Exercise may well change the way participants understand their country. Wikileaks with its leaks of secret government documents, and the way it talks about secrecy, may change how the public sees its government. The question is whether this potential is being systematically worked into traditional wisdom in nonprofit communications.

THE PROBLEM: IDEOLOGICAL GOALS ARE MISSING

In chapter 2, we talked about how the innovating ideologist closes justification gaps. Recall, justification gaps are the difference between what the current moral vocabulary is capable of justifying or condemning and what you need it to be able to justify or condemn. Closing justification gaps means more than adding a box marked "ideology" to your checklist of goals. Changing ideologies is not just a goal like any other communications goal. Ideological goals can play a fundamental role in informing all your other goals. Firstly, I will discuss why ideological change is so important to every aspect of your mission. Secondly, I will suggest how, given what Skinner says, current practices are problematic.

Ideological Change May be Vital to All Your Goals

Your nonprofit is trying to solve a problem or make the world better somehow. There are many reasons that the problem you are working on exists. Whatever it is, an important contributing factor in the equation will be how people think about your issue.

Suppose, for example, your mission is to address a rare medical

---

[50] Ongenaert, 201.

[51] *Patterson and Radtke, Strategic Communications,* xiii.

condition that is not caused or exacerbated by social conditions such as poor housing or unsafe work conditions. This condition is genetic. No group of people is disproportionately affected. This seems like a purely medical problem not an ideological problem. But, as I am sure you know, it is more difficult to raise money for rare diseases. As it turns out, ideology has a lot to do with that.

Rare diseases will consistently be less attractive to funders who have a cost-effectiveness model that seeks to maximize the number of lives potentially saved by research funding. Cost-effectiveness models are often based on controversial assumptions about how we can quantify human life and compare the value of different lives. These assumptions often go against other ways of thinking about the relative value of human life as being infinite or non-interchangeable.[52]

I hope this example shows you how even a "purely physical" issue is profoundly caught up in clashes between different social, political, and ethical philosophies and world views. According to some world views that hold quite a bit of sway in Canadian society, it makes perfect sense for rare diseases to be consistently at the back of the line.[53] If you want the rare disease you are fundraising for to be viewed differently, you will either have to argue for an exception or take on this underlying way of thinking. Both are valid communications strategies. Both aim to close the justification gap.

But the justification gap is not just about funding. A justification gap undermines your ability to accomplish all the different types of goals that strategic communications advice focuses on. Improving your organization's reputation is often a key communication goal. You have no doubt heard the advice that members of the public today like to connect with individuals rather than organizations. That is not an immutable fact of human psychology, it is a historically contingent phenomenon rooted in part in the decline of trust towards traditional

---

[52] See Michael Drummond, "Allocating Resources," *International Journal of Technology Assessment in Health Care*, 6 No 1 (January 1990): 77-92; Brock, Dan. "Ethical Issues in the Use of Cost Effectiveness Analysis for the Prioritization of Health Resources," *Handbook of Bioethics*, 78 (Dordrecht: Kluwer, 2004).

[53] See Michael D. Rawlins, Anthony J. Culyer, "National Institute for Clinical Excellence and its Value Judgments," *British Medical Journal*, (2004): 329.

institutions over the past 40 years.[54] Once upon a time, if you could describe yourself as an institution, it would inspire trust. Nowadays, it might evoke just the opposite.

Conversely, the justification gap you may be trying to remedy is between the reputation you want to have and prejudice against who you are. For example, consider the various names for the movement for people with lived experience of psychiatric institutions. They include the psychiatric survivor movement, consumer movement, ex-patient movement, and mental patients' liberation movement.[55] Each one re-frames what it means to have had experience in a mental institution. Given the prejudice against people with experience of psychiatric institutions, to get decision-makers to listen to them, members of the movement needed to reframe that experience to present it as a *qualification* rather than a *dis*qualification. Reputational goals sometimes simply cannot be accomplished without transforming language head on.

Suppose you want to inspire your employees and volunteers. Surely that is the farthest thing away from the ideological clashes and historical trends of our time. And yet, countless articles have been written about what it takes to recruit, connect with, and retain millennial staff and volunteers, and the advice is all about your mission, vision, and values.[56] So if there is a justification gap at the level of your mission, it will show up as a barrier at the level of recruitment, motivation, and retention of staff and volunteers.

All these examples show that ideological change is not just one among many goals. It can underpin the success of all your other communications goals. These justification gaps may be something you simply cope with (e.g., by doing your work without directly addressing them), or they can be something you actively take charge of and seek to resolve in your favour. And as we will discuss later, there are many ways to overcome justification gaps, ranging from leaning into them to totally rejecting them and going your own way.

---

[54] Neil Nevitte, "The Decline of Deference: Canadian Value Change" *Cross National Perspective* (Toronto: University of Toronto Press, 1996).

[55] National Empowerment Centre, "The Ex-Patients' Movement: Where We've Been and Where We're Going." *The Journal of Mind and Behavior*, 11 No 3, (Summer 1990): 323-336.

[56] "Millennials in the Nonprofit Sector," KDP Consulting.

So, let us revisit the current practices and ask how being aware of ideological goals may change your goal-setting practices.

What Ideological Transformation Means for Your Goal Setting Practices

The first implication is obviously that ideological change — changing the system of words that governs how decisions over your issues are made — should be on your communications radar.

Secondly, your communications goals do not necessarily have to be key messages that you want to explicitly communicate to the public. Rather, you may want to start with a prior goal of transforming the words that will go into your key messages, so they are capable of justifying what you are proposing. For instance, your key message might be "meat is murder" but your underlying goal might be something like "expand the reference of "murder" so that it includes killing non-human animals in order to make use of it in political, moral, and legal debate."

Thirdly, your key messages need not be jargon-free. Jargon can be at the heart of your mission. For example, "supervised injection service" is clearly more technical than "helping somebody shoot up", but it is obviously an important step away from the pejorative and stigmatizing nature of those slang terms. In the case of safe injection sites, the strategy of using jargon-y medical terms such as "health services that provide a hygienic environment" are clearly part of a broader strategy to bring the activity within the moral vocabulary of health rather than criminal law.[57]

You do not need to view yourself as being swept away by tides. What may seem natural and unstoppable may just be a deeply rooted aspect of the language we use to describe the world. The historical forces that brought our language to this point in time may be outside our control but that does not mean they are immutable. On the contrary, we are part of those forces and therefore how we speak either reflects or reinforces that status quo because we have accepted it as natural or it contributes to the ongoing process of change in a self-conscious way. Skinner emphasizes that by understanding how

---

[57] Dilshad Burman, "Toronto's safe injection sites: your FAQs answered" CityTV News, Aug 14, 2018.

the language was shaped in the first place, we better see how we can make more active choices.[58]

Paying attention to moral vocabularies also helps see what kinds of awareness raising goals are likely to lead to meaningful change. Recall that moral vocabularies consist of words that describe and judge at the same time. Consequently, your awareness raising is often implicitly making an argument. For example, you can set a goal to make 1000 people aware of homelessness in the city or set a goal to make 1000 people aware of the local housing rights crisis. Both could be described as awareness raising goals of the same underlying set of facts, but these are obviously very different goals from a communications perspective.

People already have a sense of what homelessness means and most people already accept it is a bad thing. You would think therefore that simply making them aware of it would result in change. The trouble that Skinner calls our attention to is that the problem you are trying to solve is at least compatible with the current dominant moral vocabularies to the extent that the two have co-existed until now. So, if you do not change your audience's world view, it will likely be compatible with the problem continuing to exist.

The kind of awareness that does nothing to change the moral vocabulary in which the problem or solutions are understood will therefore rarely, if ever, be enough.

How Ideological Goals May Backfire

Setting out to change moral vocabularies can lead to surprising results. So before setting ideologically transformative goals, let us explore how things can go sideways. When you set out to change moral vocabulary, how it actually changes will be out of your control. Helpfully, Skinner points to a number of specific things that might happen if your efforts fall short.

For instance, you may intend to keep the sense of a word and change its reference (i.e., the range of situations in which it can be appropriately used), but your audience fails to realize that is what you

---

[58] Quentin Skinner, *Liberty before Liberalism* (Cambridge: Cambridge University Press., 1997), 109-110.

are doing and instead thinks you are just offering a new sense.[59] They may even accept this new sense of the word, but without changing the traditional meaning. For example, the free school movement of the 1960s and 70s tried to change how society understood the proper aims of education, but largely created "alternatives" that never grew past being viewed as one of many ideas about education — and a relatively niche view at that.[60] Most of the ideas about education they challenged continue to be the norm.

You may succeed at changing the meaning of a word, but it comes at the cost of its judgment value.[61] For example, arguably this has happened to the term "state of emergency" when applied to climate change. Traditionally, an emergency is local and immediate (e.g., our house is on fire). When applied to climate change, the term "emergency" lacks this literal sense of localized and immediate danger. Through metaphor,[62] climate change advocates justify this change in meaning by arguing that the essence of an emergency is a serious danger requiring immediate action to stop it, and that this definition does apply to climate change.

At first glance, this argument would seem to be gaining traction as cities around the world declare a state of climate emergency. However, the government and public's response to the City of Toronto declaring climate change a state of emergency,[63] for example, has been nothing like the state of emergency that was declared for the Fort McMurray wildfires or COVID-19.[64] Such declarations do reflect the growing acceptance of climate change as a serious problem requiring immediate action at all levels. However, the actual responses that have followed, at least in Canada, betray the fact that advocates have not yet been successful in mobilizing the full moral force of the term "emergency"

---

[59] Skinner, *Visions of Politics*, 167.

[60] Lucas Kavner, "At Brooklyn Free School, A Movement Reborn with Liberty And No Testing For All". *The Huffington Post*. November 30, 2012.

[61] Skinner, *Visions of Politics*, 168.

[62] Thunberg Greta, "'Our house is on fire': Greta Thunberg, 16, urges leaders to act on climate," *The Guardian*, January 25, 2019.

[63] Phil Tsekouras, "City of Toronto votes unanimously to declare climate emergency," *CTV News*, October 2, 2019.

[64] The Canadian Press, "One year later: A look back at how the Fort McMurray wildfires unfolded," May 1, 2017.

with all the urgency and suspension of normal limits it conveys. This is a classic example of what Skinner describes as a split meaning word with a weakening judgment value.

THE SOLUTION: THINK BIG!

At the end of the last chapter, you built your keyword bank and drew a keyword map. In this exercise, you will define your ultimate goal in terms of this vocabulary. Think beyond what is justifiable today—beyond what is even imaginable today or acceptable as part of the normal scope of conversation—but do so using the language of today.

Firstly, as many strategic communications advisors suggest,[65] you want to get clear on what your mission actually is. Look at all the places you articulate mission (e.g., website, brochures, funding proposals, etc.). You should also ask different people inside and outside your organization what they think your mission is, including board, staff, volunteers, beneficiaries, donors, and members of the community.

Secondly, note all the discrepancies between the different versions of your mission. You don't need to worry about differences in wording, phrasing, length or anything like that yet. You are just trying to determine if everyone agrees on the substance of what you are trying to accomplish. Summarize what you think the substance of that mission is.

Thirdly, convene a meeting of the people you want to be involved in setting your organization's strategic direction. Ask them two questions:

1. **Do you agree this is the substance of what we are trying to accomplish?** If the answer is no, you must discuss and get agreement on this point first.

2. **Have we limited what we want to accomplish by what we think we can accomplish?** If the answer is yes, then identify all the assumptions you made about what is possible and all the compromises that were made in order to get various

---

[65] Brydon M. DeWitt, *The Nonprofit Development Companion: A Workbook for Fundraising Success* (Hoboken: NJ: Wiley 2010), 10.

stakeholders on board. Keep a list of all these assumptions and limitations.

The goal of this exercise is to get back to a place where you articulate what you want to accomplish free from the assumptions about what is possible. The more time you take to identify these assumptions the easier it will be to see how, before you have even started, you have already accepted that you will not challenge certain barriers.

Fourthly, after the committee meeting, take the substance of what you want to accomplish, and use conventional mission writing techniques to articulate it as a mission. Here is the catch: you can only use the keywords you identified in chapter 2's exercise (plus of course non-keywords like articles and conjunctions). You should find it difficult if not impossible to articulate your goal in existing keywords while preserving the sense, reference, and judgment value of each of these words. The final step in this exercise is to determine, for each keyword, why it fails to capture your mission. Put differently, what do you have a problem with—the sense, reference, or judgment value of each word?

At the end of this exercise, you should have a clear idea of your mission, how you have been limiting yourself, and how the current moral vocabulary around the issue is preventing you from even articulating your mission, much less accomplishing it.

Chapter 4

Organization vs Mission

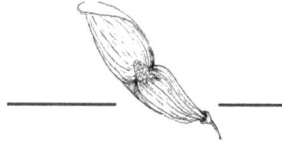

Nonprofits take a range of approaches to creating change in the world. Some take an approach that depends on the continued existence of the organization. Others take an approach that does not depend on the continued existence of the organization. Books on nonprofit communications do not distinguish between these two types of organizations. As a result, the advice is often better suited to organizations whose mission includes their continued existence. Except when individuals or institutions pursue ideological change to protect their own interests, ideological change often does not sit so comfortably with the individual or organizational interests of those who seek it.

In this chapter you will learn:

- How current advice often assumes advancing your organization advances your mission

- Cases where your organization and mission's interest part ways

- How to articulate the justifications for your mission in a way that doesn't innovate more than necessary.

CONVENTIONAL WISDOM: IDENTIFYING ORGANIZATION WITH MISSION

There is pretty much a consensus among nonprofit communications strategists that good strategic communications must begin with your mission.[66]

But where does that leave the interests of your organization in a communications strategy? Is your mission the sole point of reference for decision-making, or is organizational well-being also a factor? Are these two the same thing?

The ambiguity of your organization's relationship to your mission plays out most vitally when you need to define your stakeholders and target audience. You might be advised to focus exclusively on people and institutions who can make the change you want to see, which implicitly references your mission.[67] You might also be advised to define target audiences primarily in terms of their relationship to the organization rather than the mission, such as donors, funders, and those who influence them.[68] You could be advised to do a bit of both, appealing to those who "influence your nonprofit and its mission most", leaving it open to interpretation whether these are always the same people or two different groups.[69]

While these three positions may overlap, they are not all saying the same thing.

If you are a nonprofit housing organization, the people who can make the change you want to see might be different levels of government and maybe real estate developers and other market actors. Those stakeholders who have an influence over your organization also expand the list to include members, funders and donors. Donors and beneficiaries and those who have an influence over them may include community members, tenants, and even your local church.

---

[66] See Kinzey, *Promoting nonprofits*, 20; Brinckerhoff, *Mission-based marketing*, 2; Patterson and Radtke, *Strategic Communications*, xiv; DeWitt, *Nonprofit Development Companion,* 7-10; Conrardy, "Build a Better Nonprofit Marketing Plan: Here's How." *Prosper Strategies,* 2018.

[67] *The Communications Plan,* SaskCulture.

[68] Upleaf Technology Solutions, *Upleaf nonprofit communications plan template* (n.d.).

[69] Conrardy, *Build a Better Nonprofit Marketing Plan,* 66.

One consistent piece of advice in strategic communications is to be as specific as possible in defining target audiences.[70] It therefore makes a great deal of practical difference how you think of the relationship between your organization's interests and your mission.

It seems to me that most communications advice assumes that to advance the organization is to advance the mission, so what is good for the organization is good for the mission.

A marketer might say, "Of course, you should always start with your mission. It's the reason your organization exists, and *it's the most valuable asset you have in marketing*" (emphasis added).[71] This commercial marketing approach is likely to only become more influential as "branding" does in the nonprofit sector.[72] Talking about the mission as an asset may be practical and realistic from a branding and trademarks perspective, but it nevertheless inverts the relationship between the organization and the mission. The mission is positioned as a crucial asset for the survival and prosperity of the organization, instead of the organization as something that serves the mission.

In this vein, strategists sometimes encourage board members and staff to adopt a sense of "ownership" over the organization's issues.[73] People might use the language of "ownership" when they want to promote a sense of responsibility. They might feel that the sense of control and identification that is supposed to come along with ownership will incentivize taking responsibility. The result, however, in using this literally appropriative language is more than a mere transference of responsibility. It conveys that not only should the organization identify as much as possible with its mission, but tacitly, that the mission should be identified with the organization, its board, and its staff. The issue "belongs" to them and *is* them in some sense.

---

[70] Williams, David, *Marketing & Communications in Nonprofit Organizations: It Matters More Than You Think, Essays on Excellence* (Centre for Nonprofit Leadership and Georgetown University), 2009, 10 – 11.

[71] Brinckerhoff, *Mission-based marketing*, 2.

[72] Williams, 10-11.

[73] MissionBox staff, "Drafting a Nonprofit Communications Strategy," April 1, 2020.

Indeed, branding an organization as the issue itself makes organizational survival central to its communications. [74]

Assuming that advancing the organization necessarily means advancing the mission has several practical consequences for how you plan strategic communications and use language. It informs your choice and prioritization of issues. For example, according to Warren Mason, a professor of business and communication studies at Plymouth State University in New Hampshire, strategic communication means responding to "issues that might jeopardize an organization's very survival".[75] It informs what you emphasize in your communications For example, David Williams, another communications professor and veteran nonprofit communications professional, emphasizes the need to communicate how your organization's services are distinctive.[76] Your key messages become not so much what you want people to remember about your issue but about your nonprofit (and what it is doing to address that issue).[77] Strategic communications becomes about promoting ongoing engagement, not necessarily with the issue but with the organization.[78]

Relatedly, and understandably, works on fundraising emphasize that fundraising is always a goal of all nonprofit communications,[79] and the needs and interests of funders and donors become crucial in informing the content of your communications.[80] This also has major implications for the amount and types of communication. As David Williams has observed:

> *"More than anything, pressures from development account for the proliferation of publications across the nonprofit sector. Our organizations are clogged with annual reports, magazines,*

---

[74] Wiggill, Marlene. "Strategic communication management in the nonprofit sector: a simplified model," *Journal of Public Affairs*, 11 No 4 (2011): 226-235; "What Is Strategic Communications?" IDEA (March 16, 2011); Williams, 10-11.

[75] Wiggill, 10-11.

[76] Williams, *Marketing & Communications*, 2.

[77] Conrardy, *Build a Better Nonprofit Marketing Plan*, 66.

[78] Dayton English, "Strategic Communication Objectives for Nonprofit Organizations", Chron (n.d.).

[79] Kinzey, *Promoting Nonprofits*, 43.

[80] Brinckerhoff, *Mission Based Marketing*, 6.

newsletters, case statements, working papers and brochures targeted at planned givers, annual givers, alumni givers, givers of every sort." [81]

Ultimately, according to this view, you want to promote a "positive" image of the organization[82] that encourages people to trust you.[83] As Dayton English, a Calgary-based nonprofit communications professional, insightfully put it, "As a nonprofit organization, familiarizing the public with your work and the importance of the work you do establishes an ongoing business case for supporting your nonprofit."[84] Consequently, how you use your words must therefore be informed by what kind of personality you want your organization to have.[85]

THE PROBLEM: ADVANCING ORGANIZATION AND MISSION ARE NOT THE SAME

When it comes to ideological change, we cannot assume that what is in your organization's interests will necessarily advance your mission. Below we will look at cases where the interests of the organization and mission are separate and even conflicting.

Advancing Organization Can Undermine Mission

Quentin Skinner's studies of how ideologies change are rarely concerned with particular organizations, in part because there was no nonprofit sector, as we understand it today, during the times of the Renaissance and Reformation. The kinds of actors he studied include governments, churches, classes, and individual writers. Although he did not always use this word, in a colloquial sense, we could call what Skinner studied political and intellectual "movements", as well as the key writers who contributed to them. This is important because it reminds us that while each actor may have been acting in their own

---

[81] Williams, *Marketing & Communications*, 10-11.

[82] Patterson and Radtke, *Strategic Communications*, 3.

[83] English, "Strategic Communication Objectives for Nonprofit Organizations".

[84] English, "Strategic Communication Objectives for Nonprofit Organizations." It is telling that this article was written for a website that primarily deals with a wide range of general interest and business matters.

[85] CallHub, "4 Steps For An Effective Nonprofit Communications Strategy," CallHub (2020).

interest to some extent,[86] their individual contributions were significant because of how they contributed to a larger movement.

The question is, therefore, to what extent will pursuing what is in the best interests of your nonprofit as an organization promote or hinder your contributions to broader movements? For example, let's look at the idea that it is in the interest of your organization to define your services distinctively. From an organizational perspective, this makes a lot of sense. You want to carve out a niche for yourself, so you stand out in the marketplace for funders and donors. Niche marketing, however, often misses the point that the fate of a particular issue is often ultimately caught in such a wide network of meanings that a much larger issue is really at stake.

For example, in the 1200s, the city-states of Northern Italy asserted their independence from the Holy Roman Empire but lacked a legal foundation for doing so.[87] Ultimately, it was a much more general reversal of the idea that the facts had to follow the law, rather than vice versa, that grounded the case of the Italian city-states. Once this broad reversal happened, the city-states could then point to the fact that they were independent in practice to justify their independence in law. A more modern example would be environmental organizations dedicated to a single species or conversation area whose communications about the local may obscure the global interconnected nature of the environment.

Andrea Smith in *The Revolution Will Not Be Funded* argues that niche marketing focuses you more and more on specific issues and takes you away from the bigger picture; the result is not a mass-based movement but an aggregate of specialists.[88] Smith's insights are reflective of the general tension between the ongoing professionalization of the sector on the one hand and the voluntary, grassroots, civil society, or social movement bodies from which nonprofit

---

[86] Quentin Skinner, "III. Some Problems in the Analysis of Political Thought and Action," *Political Theory*, 2 No. 3 (August 1, 1974): 108, 197.

[87] Quentin Skinner, *The Foundations of Modern Political Thought* (Cambridge: Cambridge University Press, 1978), 8-9.

[88] INCITE! (Ed.). *The Revolution Will Not Be Funded: Beyond the Non-Profit Industrial Complex* (London: Duke University Press, 2007), 11.

organizations often emerge.[89] From the perspective of the professional vision of the sector, grassroots organizations are often viewed as simply less developed versions of professional organizations, as opposed to something different.[90] On the one hand, it is true that grassroots organizations often lack technical expertise, and that this hampers them as an organization, but to end the story there is to miss the full picture.

Peter Frumkin, a nonprofit leadership scholar at the University of Pennsylvania, identifies *two* functions of the nonprofit sector: instrumental *and* expressive. The instrumental function of the nonprofit sector is to address social problems through increasingly improved technical methods based on professionalism and expertise.[91] But civil society groups focus more on empowering stakeholders by validating and valuing (some might say emancipating) their non-expert lived experience.[92] Civil society does not improve through technical refinement but through the expression of voices and values, so that they get their due in collective decision-making.

Frumkin observed that the professionalization of the sector was part of a broader tendency to favour the service functions of the sector over its expressive and advocacy roles. Valuing expertise at the expense of lived experience is dangerous because no amount of technical perfection can replace the justice that is intrinsically achieved by people playing an active role in the decisions that affect their lives.

Andrea Smith states that Thunder Hawk of Women of All Red Nations observed that experts "are generally not part of the communities they advocate for and hence do not contribute to building grassroots leadership, particularly in indigenous communities."[93] Said

---

[89] Amanda Stewart, "Understanding nonprofit professionalization: Common concepts and new directions for research," (Student Paper, American University, 2014): 2.

[90] Clare McWatt, Melina Condren, "From the Bottom Up: A Growth Strategy for Grassroots Groups in Ontario. Grassroots Growth," Volunteer Toronto, (2017).

[91] Stewart, "Understanding nonprofit professionalization"; Peter Frumkin, *On Being Nonprofit: A Conceptual and Policy Primer*, (Cambridge, MA: Harvard University Press, 2005).

[92] Benjamin Miller, "The People and the Experts: What Each Knows and What it Means for Politics," *Half a Maven* (January 22, 2018).

[93] INCITE!, ed., 10.

differently, certain kinds of change will never be able to be achieved by certain kinds of communicating.

The expressive and technical elements of the sector need not be in tension, however. Consider for example the AIDS activist group ACT UP. In its early days, it was highly effective at garnering attention, transforming the word "AIDS" itself into a watchword for political and pharmaceutical decision-makers, whereas before they could get away with not even saying it.[94] And yet, this did not translate to results until they could accompany it with a more targeted identification of the roadblocks in pharmaceutical production. The grassroots and technical expertise needed one another.

But this way of talking about the two facets of the sector should not fool us into thinking that the grassroots is political and the technical is apolitical. The systematic application of Skinner's method quickly reveals that as a pitfall. Technical issues, such as a drug development process, are always anchored in underlying political notions of, for example, what an institution believes it is capable of doing. For instance, around the time that universities in Canada began responding to COVID-19 by shifting all classes online, my sister told me about a friend of hers who had to drop out of university just a few months earlier because her request for accommodation of a disability through remote classes was deemed impossible. People with disabilities often face political issued presented as technical ones.

It is not that there are no technical problems. All the political will in the world will not help you if you have not properly thought through and crafted a solution to address the facts on the ground. Nevertheless, all the political will in the world *will* switch people's thinking from "whether" to "how" and that makes all the difference. The point is that it is not only possible but often necessary for expertise and community power to work collaboratively to both go beyond the limits of what seems currently possible.

But there are risks. When an organization describes its mission as its most valuable asset, for example, it may literally be appropriating someone else's struggles for its own bottom line (understood in terms

---

[94] Aizenman, Nurith, "How To Demand A Medical Breakthrough: Lessons From The AIDS Fight," *National Public Radio* (February 9, 2019).

of the value of its "brand equity"). When it defines ongoing engagement of its audience in terms of ongoing engagement *with the organization* rather than the issue, it is making itself an intermediary and thereby fostering dependence of its stakeholders on it.

How can Quentin Skinner's method help practice strategic communications in a way that is more accountable to the stakeholders you serve? It obviously cannot replace members of the community taking roles of leadership in your organization, and your organization's ongoing accountability to those communities' collective vision(s) and needs as articulated in dialogue with them.[95] What Quentin Skinner's method can offer is the benefit of a rigorous technical process that de-centres the organization, and thereby avoids many of the pitfalls mentioned above.

For example, according to my reading of Skinner's method, your target audience should begin with those who hold the power to make the change sought. This may mean the government, or, if you believe that the existing institutions themselves are the barriers to change, the people who you believe must be the source of the new institutions. Your primary audience, however, will almost by definition never be funders or donors, although it may be your members or the people you serve.

Advancing Mission May Not Advance the Organization

We saw in the first part of this chapter that the goal of strategic communications is often to get people to know more about your organization. However, if you limit yourself to communicating only in ways that make the organization more memorable, you will miss the fact that the most successful linguistic change is often ultimately anonymous.

Consider the meaning of the word "pride" in contemporary Canadian political vocabulary. In its common uses, this word has many positive associations,[96] such as "I am proud of you" or "I am proud of my accomplishments." It is also strongly linked to LGBTQ issues

---

[95] Miller, Benjamin. "Theorizing Legal Needs: Towards a Caring Legal System." (Thesis, University of Ottawa, 2016), 47-48.

[96] It would be difficult to say it has exclusively positive connotations, since there is a history of "pride" being viewed as a vice, e.g., "pride comes before a fall".

through the Pride Parade, which in recent years has been attended by over a million people.[97] However, do you know who organized the first Pride Parade in Canada? Do you know which organizations put in the work to maintain it over decades when it was far less popular and even dangerous? Of the millions of people who understand the word "pride" as linked to LGBTQ issues, only a relatively small portion know how this connection was forged in Canada.

The four organizations who organized the first Canadian Pride Parade were the University of Toronto Homophile Association, Toronto Gay Action (Now)[98] and the Community Homophile Association of Toronto.[99] The University of Toronto Homophile Association, formed in 1969, disbanded only a few years later in 1973. Yet from the perspective of the early development of the movement, especially in Ontario, it played an influential role.[100] Toronto Gay Action never had more than a dozen or so members, but most went on to form the core group of the highly influential magazine the Body Politic.[101] Born out of the University of Toronto Homophile Association, The Community Homophile Association of Toronto had a similarly brief but colourful organizational history.[102]

Seen through the lens of Skinner's theory, nonprofits can make a large contribution without even surviving or being very large, much less having those accomplishments attracting the public's attention to those organizations. The point is that, for many kinds of ideological changes, no single organization has to be the one to do it. In a healthy, fluid, and flexible movement, people will be able to carry on the work of one organization with others under another banner. Indeed, in the case of Community Homophile Association of Toronto, it seems from the brief historical reflection cited above that the dependence on a single organization was quite detrimental to the community.

---

[97] Pride Toronto. "Pride Toronto: Economic Impact Report 2019" (2019): 4.

[98] This part of the name is sometimes included and often left out.

[99] Pride in Canada, *The Canadian Encyclopedia* (June 28, 2016).

[100] "Heritage plaque honours Ontario's first gay and lesbian rights group," *U of T News* (November 3, 2011).

[101] Jearld Frederick Moldenhauer, "Toronto Gay Action, The Gay Alliance Toward Equality and CHAT" (n.d.).

[102] CHAT (Community Homophile Association of Toronto), Bits And Pieces (n.d.).

Advancing Mission May Undermine Organization

Another example of ideological change is the history of the terms used for Black people in America. In the 60s, Black organizations had already spent decades promoting the use of the term "Negro" over more pejorative and over-inclusive alternatives such as "coloured", because they saw it as a term connoting hope for progress and self-help.[103] However, it came under attack as being imposed on Black people by White people, implying subservence and "Uncle-Tomism".[104] Radical and militant groups such as the Black Muslims and Black Panthers actively favoured "Black", in part because, as an antonym to White, it supported Black separatist ideas and stood for "racial pride, militancy, power, and rejection of the status quo".[105] They actively grappled with the negative connotations of the term "black" that existed in the dominant moral vocabulary, and countered with slogans like "Black is beautiful" and "Black pride" and they were largely and quickly successful, particularly among college students.[106] These campaigns illustrate the kind of political-linguistic sensitivities highlighted in Chapter 2.

Similarly, in the late 80s, the National Urban Coalition (NUC) actively promoted "African-American" to replace "Black", because, they argued, this new term aligned their communities with other ethnic communities, gave African-Americans a sense of their roots from which they had been cut off, and located their issues in a global dialogue.[107] Though the NUC preferred a very different way of organizing from the Black Panthers and Black Muslims, they were clearly attuned to the way moral vocabulary facilitates or hinders different kinds of organizing.

As with "pride" above, when most people use the term "Black" or "African-American", most are likely unaware of the histories behind them. The ultimate popular meaning of a word is never singular and is rarely identical with what proponents intend. But, decades later, we

---

[103] Tom W. Smith, "Changing Racial Labels: From 'Colored' to 'Negro' to 'Black' to 'African American,'" *The Public Opinion Quarterly* 56 no. 4 (1992): 497.

[104] Smith, 499.

[105] Smith, 499.

[106] Smith, 501-502.

[107] Smith, 503.

observe how effective these linguistic campaigns were at providing language that continues to facilitate the kind of organizing methodologies and assumptions their initial proponents envisioned. Consider for example Black Lives Matter.

In one sense, the Black Panthers taking this posture did not serve their organizational interests since many of their members were assassinated, and besides that their activities were under constant surveillance.[108] It is doubtful, however, whether their approach and the kind of changes they were proposing could ever have been undertaken by any organization primarily concerned with its own reputation and longevity. And yet, in some sense the promotion of the term Black did also promote the organizations behind it, including the Black Panthers, but not because people know the connection between the two. This highlights an important point. Even when we de-centre the organizational interest, it does not completely disappear. The actors Skinner calls innovating ideologists do act out of self-interest. The point is rather that if we take the nonprofit's mission seriously, we cannot simply assume that the survival and prosperity of the organization is identical with the advancement of the mission. In this way, branding may well sometimes be self-defeating when you are trying to innovate ideologically.

In the first section of this chapter, we talked about how communications reflect your organization's desired personality. Did the Black Panthers therefore advocate for the use of the term "Black" because it accorded well with their organizational personality, or did that "personality" flow logically from their reading of what kind of action was needed for Black liberation? It is telling in this regard that the Black Panthers often changed their rhetoric, both as a response to killings and jail sentences and to continuously appeal to "the people".[109] They had a sense of becoming the organization they believed their community needed.

---

[108] Jeffrey Haas, *The assassination of Fred Hampton: How the FBI and the Chicago police murdered a Black Panther* (Chicago: Lawrence Hill Books/Chicago Review Press, 2010).

[109] Gwendolyn D. Pough, "Empowering Rhetoric: Black Students Writing Black Panthers," *College Composition and Communication*, 53 No. 3 (Feb. 2002): 470.

When it comes to doing a situation analysis, we must realize that understanding the strengths, weaknesses, opportunities, and threats to an organization in terms of the organization's ability to operate is not the same as understanding the strengths, weaknesses, opportunities, and threats to the position that the organization has determined it needs to take. For instance, viewed strictly from the organization's perspective, several offers of major grants may be viewed as opportunities. And yet, when viewed from the position's perspectives, these offers may represent threats to the organization's autonomy and ability to assume positions that are unpalatable to the funders but needed according to the organization's analysis of the justification gap.

I hope I have shown three things in the above discussion. Firstly, you can advance your organization in ways that undermine your mission, for example, when you specialize to the point that you lose sight of the bigger picture. Secondly, you can advance your cause without necessarily advancing your organization, so you should not assume that you need to do the latter to do the former. This is shown by how small and short-lived organizations have sometimes had out-sized impact on broader movements. This is important because it means your energies may be misdirected towards the continuity of your organization when that is not necessarily what your mission needs at that moment. Thirdly, advancing your mission may entail taking a posture which is actively bad for your organization, such as when it is highly controversial or adversarial.

This might sound like the old refrain of "put your mission before your own interests." This may seem like just another version of the same old ideas about altruism that have devalued the work of women and people of colour in the sector for so long. This is a real risk of any analysis that focuses exclusively on the mission without regard for the long-term well-being of staff. In an ethics of care, the well-being of the caregiver matters just as the care recipient. I am not saying that you, the caregiver, do not matter. Rather, I am saying that the interests of caregiver and care recipient should not be confused. Organizational well-being may be a politically valuable goal, but it is a distinct one and that means you must be aware of the tension that might arise between that goal and the advancement of your mission.

Because the accomplishment of your mission and the interests of your staff may be distinct, it may be helpful to have an organizational philosophy that encompasses both and explain how they relate to one another. Skinner's method is not a replacement for conventional strategic communications tools that look after your organization's interests. Rather, *The 100-Year PR Plan* is a complementary tool meant to focus goals reflecting a longer vision.

THE SOLUTION: RE-CENTRING YOUR MISSION

In Chapter 3's exercise you articulated your mission with the keywords identified in chapter 2's exercise. In this exercise, we will articulate the arguments you are using to support your mission in keywords.

Gathering Your Current Justifications

Firstly, you want to get clear on the basic arguments you make for why your mission should be accomplished. Look at all the places you articulate arguments for your mission (e.g., website, brochures, funding proposals, etc.). You should also ask different people inside and outside your organization why they think your mission is important, including, board, staff, volunteers, beneficiaries, donors, and members of the community. Record all these arguments in a table like the following:

Source	Argument Content	Argument Type
www.postgrowth.org Home page	"Imagine your great grand-children thriving, here on planet Earth."	Appeal to self-interest/ interpersonal relationships
www.postgrowth.org Home page	"While our extractive, growth-dependent economy is driving us to collapse, a full circle, post-growth economy is emerging, offering a pathway to our shared thriving within ecological limits."	Appeal to material/moral ideal of collective life ("shared thriving")
www.postgrowth.org Home page	"At the Post Growth Institute, our goal is to help guide the way to that more beautiful world your heart knows is possible."	Appeal to aesthetics ("beautiful world") Appeal to intuition ("your heart knows")

Secondly, once you stop seeing new types of arguments, group them by type. In a committee with those responsible for your organization's strategic direction, order the argument types according to how fundamental they are to you.

Thirdly, compare the language you have used in your past materials to the keywords in the word map you created. Are you using words in a way that shares the same sense, reference, and judgment? Where are the main points of disagreement? These will likely be the places that your arguments are most implausible or considered a stretch.

The final step is to tidy up your justifications, so they are:

- succinct,
- articulated as much as possible in the current common keywords, and
- written in a way that is compelling to your audience, not you.

Be Succinct

In his Lectures on Ethics, John Dewey, the great American philosopher of education, science, and liberalism, once wrote something to the effect that entire books are written so that a single line should be disseminated into the public consciousness.[110] It seems to me that this idea is obviously reflected in Skinner's approach to studying the contribution of great works of political theory to ideological change. Consider for example, the popular protest sign "Liberty or Death" which is taken from a quotation attributed to Patrick Henry from a speech he made in 1775.[111] Similarly, though apparently erroneously attributed to Gandhi, the expression "Be the change you want to see in the world" is another example of a book most people have forgotten but a phrase that has long lived on.[112]

Think of ideas as the blood of the body politic. To the greatest

---

[110] Unfortunately, I cannot find the source for this idea. I read this many years ago and have often thought about it since but can never find where I read it. Only now do I realize how ironic that is.

[111] David Kilcullen, "Home of the hateful, fearful, heavily armed," *The Australian*, May 30, 2020; James D. Hart, Philip Leininger, *The Oxford Companion to American Literature* (Oxford: Oxford University Press,1995), 286.

[112] "Be the Change You Wish to See in the World," https://quoteinvestigator.com/2017/10/23/be-change/.

extent possible, you want to be thinking about what the state of that blood will be by the time it has circulated through the whole body. Indeed, several strategic communications advisors observe how frequently people disagree within an organization over what the mission statement even says (much less what it means).[113] You want to write your justifications in a way that has the best possible chance of preserving your intention throughout their circulation in the public consciousness. This starts with being succinct.

Consequently, at this stage in formulating your 100-year plan it is important to formulate your justification as succinctly as possible. This is not quite a process of stringing together slogans, nor is it merely listing key messages. Rather, it is a process of articulating the big picture rationale for the change you are proposing. Examples of justifications include:

- We need to stop using fossil fuels because if we do not the planet will become uninhabitable.

- We need to end the abuse of women because women are people too.

- Seat belts should be legally required in all cars in order to save lives.

A word of warning about being succinct. Now more than ever, there is pressure from social media, and the sound-bite culture of traditional media, to never really go beyond this high-level form of communication. Consider the case of the Lance Armstrong Foundation and the LiveStrong bracelets.[114] Although the bracelets quickly became wildly popular, the energy wasn't directed towards anything that specifically advanced their mission.

Failing to go deeper in both your thinking and your communications is a recipe for shallowness. Sometimes you need whole books to change the meaning of a single word, but then, and only then, will you be able to change someone's mind with only a few words. This exercise is dedicated to finding the starting point for those few words, whereas later exercises will be about "the books".

---

[113] DeWitt, *Nonprofit Development*, p.10.
[114] Williams, Marketing and Communications, 12.

Articulate Your Justifications in the Current Moral Vocabulary

The difference between the words you are currently using to make your arguments and the current common moral vocabulary is the innovation you are already pursuing. The purpose of this exercise is to ensure you do not innovate more than you need to. As Einstein is sometimes purported to have said, "Everything should be made as simple as possible, but no simpler." The corollary here is "Be as innovative as you need to be, but no more innovative." The boldness that a 100-year plan allows for is possible in part because you do not need to do everything at once. That is why it is so importance that you begin with trying to articulate your justifications in current keywords.

It's not meant to encourage "patience" or slow reform for its own sake. Rather, when you strategically deploy resources over the long-term, be mindful of the costs of innovating too much at once. You may well want to shock your audience, but to be shocked they must first understand.

Consider the P2P (Peer to Peer) Foundation's Report "P2P Accounting for Planetary Survival".[115] The Report starts off with a warning that the bulk of the report is for the motivated expert.[116] This is a fair warning to non-experts about later chapters. However, even in its introductory chapter for the non-expert, the Report articulates its vision through several fascinating linguistic innovations, including:

- Cosmo-local production or DGML
- Economies of scope
- Perma-circular economies
- Ecosystemic ledgers
- Metabolic streams
- Netarchical capitalism,
- Mammon.[117]

To be fair to the authors, they do a good job of explaining these terms, and they each capture genuinely distinct concepts for which

---

[115] Michel Bauwens, Alex Pazaitis, "P2P Accounting for Planetary Survival," P2P Foundation, 2019.

[116] Bauwens and Pazaitis, 8.

[117] Bauwens and Pazaitis, 18-22.

existing language would be clunky and inadequate. Nevertheless, every word imposes a cost on the listener, reader, and future writer who wants to quote them, and must explain it, remember it, integrate it into their vocabulary.

Plain language expert Iva Cheung calls this cost to the audience "cognitive load".[118] Both for strategic reasons and out of fairness to those on whom your communications impose the cost, you should minimize cognitive load to what is strictly required to accomplish your goal. If the only way to articulate your justification requires background knowledge, time, or attention that your audience may not have, then one of at least three things will happen:

- It simply will not reach your audience.
- It will reach your audience but only through intermediaries, such as media, teachers, bloggers or artists.
- It will only reach a relatively limited number of people who are especially dedicated or else have the resources to get to where you are in understanding.[119]

How much the words you use deviate from how your audience currently uses words can therefore play an important role in dictating the shape and size of the broader movement you can catalyze or be integrated into, as well as who has power in that movement (e.g., who the intermediaries are).

That brings us back to thinking about how the experts should be relating to the grassroots. The short answer is that for the purpose of crafting your 100-year plan, you start where your audience is. Start by going to them in order to understand whether and how they will be able to reach you.

Be Compelling from Your Audience's Point of View

Your reasons for supporting your mission may be very different from the reasons that might move your audience to support it. As we will

---

[118] I.W. Cheung, "Plain language to minimize cognitive load: A social justice perspective," *IEEE Transactions on Professional Communication*, 60 No 4 (2017): 448-457.

[119] Benjamin Miller, "The Intrusion of Real Life into Philosophy: The Pedagogical, Methodological, and Political Implications of Acknowledging we Have Other Stuff Going On," *Half a Maven* (2018).

see in the next chapter, most strategic communications advice counsels you to focus on what your audience wants. For the same reason that you should start with words that your audience understands, this makes good sense. This is only a beginning.

Bring it All Together

Suppose a group of community members get together online in response to COVID-19. They have seen the news about, and may even have personal experience of, the horrors that go on in long-term care homes.[120] They believe everyone should receive the excellent quality care that they need regardless of their financial means and whether there are people in their lives who are able and willing to advocate for their needs.

This vision seems so obvious to them that, at first, they do not think about why this goal is justified. But then they remember that despite the fact that everyone would have agreed with this goal before COVID-19, we still have the system we have. They realize that major changes are going to be needed and they are probably going to take much longer than the current outrage and attention will last, especially given the fast-changing global situation.

After much discussion, they settle on the idea that everyone has a right to be treated with dignity and would they ever want their loved ones to have to live in circumstances like that? They figure that this appeal to the language of the Universal Declaration of Human Rights is both true to how they feel and will be easily recognizable to people. They add the part about loved ones because they reason that ultimately what makes this issue so emotional is how personal it is. They draft the following statement: "Every senior should receive excellent care regardless of their financial means because we all have a right to age with dignity and would not want to see our loved ones receive any less."

---

[120] Adam Carter, "Military report reveals what sector has long known: Ontario's nursing homes are in trouble," *CBC Toronto*, May 27, 2020.

Chapter 5

The Customer is Not Always Right

"Our will is always for our own good, but we do not always see what that is."

—Jean-Jacques Rousseau

In the first section of this chapter, I will discuss the conventional wisdom which says to target your customer, identify what they want, and give it to them. In the second part, we will see how Skinner's method shows us your ultimate audience may not be who you think it is. Ultimately, in the third section, I will discuss how to identify this hidden audience.

In this chapter you will learn:

- That you should always be implicitly addressing the silent opposition who maintain the dominant ideological structures
- How to identify a decision-maker's justification for their actions without them explaining
- How to identify the silent opposition.

CONVENTIONAL WISDOM: THE CUSTOMER IS ALWAYS RIGHT

Current communications advice involves identifying your audience, discovering their wants through research, and giving them what they want in your communications.

Defining Your Target Audience

Strategic communications advice starts with a reminder that there is no "general public", and even if there were, you would not have the resources to reach them all. You need to narrow down your audiences as much as possible and prioritize.[121] This will force you to make some tough choices.[122] The question therefore is how do you define your audiences and then how do you prioritize them?

It seems that no two books or articles on strategic communications, fundraising, or marketing take the same approach to this question, though there is much overlap. Ruth Ellen Kinzey, author of *Promoting Nonprofit Organizations: A Reputational Management Approach*, talks about taking an inventory of the nonprofit "publics", asking questions such as "who do you want to communicate with? Who should you communicate with? Have critical audiences been overlooked?"[123] She gives examples of potential audiences ranging from state regulators and bloggers to foundations and donors. Venessa Bowers, owner of a PR firm specializing in arts organizations, states that since most nonprofits are funded by corporations, foundations, and governments, they must be able to communicate with these decision-makers.[124]

Marlene Wiggill, senior lecturer at Lund University specializing in strategic communications, comments that most nonprofits view donors as their first priority.[125] David Williams, an advisor with decades of experience, explains that you must start with your mission and ask: what do I need to make progress, focusing on both those who support or could oppose you?[126] You must be as specific as possible otherwise

---

[121] Patterson and Radtke, *Strategic Communication*, 65; Williams, *Marketing & Communications*, 9; Kinzey, *Promoting nonprofits*, 31.

[122] Williams, *Marketing & Communications*, 9.

[123] Kinzey, *Promoting nonprofits*, 31.

[124] Wiggill, *Strategic communication management*, 226.

[125] Wiggill, 227.

[126] Williams, 10-11.

it will be difficult to target your message to your group.[127] Similarly, SaskCulture, a nonprofit that supports cultural organizations in Saskatchewan, recommends being as specific as possible in thinking about who can deliver the change you seek.[128]

Sally Patterson and Janel Radtke, two experienced advisors, say in their well-known seven-step strategic planning process that a non-profit should focus on those who can help them advance their mission. They then proceed to segment the public into three groups: the active public (those already taking action on an issue), the engaged public (those who know about the issue and may become ready to act), informed public (those aware of the problem but not necessarily what is being done or could be done).[129]

They recommend targeting them in that order, since a nonprofit should focus on who they are most likely to reach. They also provide a useful worksheet for identifying critical stakeholders. This includes organizations doing similar work, people and organizations that oppose your work, funders, donors, community leaders, media, and government, as well as many other potential stakeholders.[130] They identify outreach partners, those who can influence the audience you want to influence.[131]

Understanding Your Target Audience

After narrowing and prioritizing your target audience, the next most consistent piece of advice is that you need to understand your audience as much as possible.[132] This is necessary in order to develop more resonant messages, understand how your audience will react, and give you an edge in the crowded marketplace of messages.[133] The question therefore is what do you need to know about your audience?

---

[127] Williams, 10-11.

[128] SaskCulture, "The Communications Plan".

[129] Patterson and Radtke, 65.

[130] Patterson and Radtke, 61-64.

[131] Patterson and Radtke, 68.

[132] Wiggill, 226; Patterson and Radtke, 68-69; MissionBox Staff, "Drafting a Nonprofit Communications Strategy," April 1, 2020.

[133] Network for Good, "How to Define Your Target Audience: Is Your Nonprofit a Match for Your Community?" June 22, 2010.

The answer for some is simply as much as possible.[134] Ultimately, you want to be able to "stand in their shoes",[135] which includes understanding what makes them tick, their problems and prejudices, their feelings about your organization, its issues, programs and services.[136] A stakeholder "persona" can be created, embodying the characteristics, thoughts, feeling, and actions of a representative blend of your community.[137] You can determine those thoughts, feeling and actions by researching your audience's demographic, such as age, sex, income bracket, and psychographic characteristics, such as desires, self-concept, and lifestyle.[138] Understanding how motivations of segments of your audience differ is important. Understanding policymakers, for example, means understanding their commitment to their constituents and their broader policy agenda.[139] How your audience ranks your issues relative to others and is important and how they react to different words and phrases.[140]

The goal, according to conventional wisdom, is to create an emotional connection.[141] Indeed, for-profit businesses have long recognized this and used it to their advantage in their marketing.[142] Some recognize that what works in business does not always apply to nonprofits.[143]

Appreciating your audience's emotions will likely lead you to a couple of conclusions. It is better to personalize asks, because they prefer to have a personal relationship with the organization.[144] This

---

[134] Network for Good.

[135] Patterson and Radtke, 68-69.

[136] Patterson and Radtke, 68-69.

[137] Conrardy, Build a Better Nonprofit Marketing Plan, 66.

[138] Patterson and Radtke, 69-70.

[139] Patterson and Radtke at p.68.

[140] Williams at p.11.

[141] Davenport, Debra, *Strategic Communication Impact on the Nonprofit Sector,* Brian Lamb School of Communication, Purdue University, n.d.

[142] Baobao Song & Jing Taylor Wen, "Online corporate responsibility communications strategies and stakeholder engagements: A comparison of controversial versus non-controversial industries," *Corporate Social Responsibility and Environmental Management,* 2019.

[143] idea.org, "What is strategic communications?".

[144] Kinzey, Promoting Nonprofits, 5.

also means maintaining that personal relationship over time, by keeping them regularly updated and not just calling on them when you need something.[145] Also, emotions are key to strategic nonprofit storytelling.[146] For the same reason that you personalize your ask, you personalize your story: who is affected? What peril are they facing? How can your correspondent help? What will they achieve? Why should they do it? How will it make them feel? According to this line of thinking, this is how to make your message memorable.[147]

Giving Your Audience What it Wants

Once you know who your audience is and you understand them thoroughly, the next piece of advice given is to craft your communications to meet their needs. You want to treat your audience like valued customers.[148] The most basic level of communications practices, requires you to make your issues "relevant" to the audience. David Williams highlights this lesson with the following story about the National Audubon Society, a birding organization facing decreasing populations of some bird species:[149]

> *"...in the early 1990s...the organization's new leadership decided that Audubon needed to take a much more aggressive political posture (about environmental issues that affected birds). They ditched the revered whooping crane logo ("the bird image hurts us," the CEO said at the time), fired the veteran editor of their signature magazine, and launched the kind of political activist campaigns usually associated with the Sierra Club. But that wasn't what Audubon members wanted. They were birders. They liked the crane. They wanted the magazine full of handsome photographs of warblers, not partisan screeds on toxic waste. The defections were swift, and Audubon's membership and fundraising dropped sharply. Finally, the board had to*

---

[145] Mark Hager, Elizabeth Searing. "10 Ways to Kill Your Nonprofit," *Nonprofit Quarterly*, (Winter 2014).

[146] Pete Mackey, "The 'Five P's' of Strategic Nonprofit Storytelling", *Storytelling Procedures*, February 12, 2018.

[147] Williams, *Marketing and Communications*, 3.

[148] Brinckerhoff, *Mission-based Marketing*, 3.

[149] Williams, *Marketing and Communications*, 3.

act, and the CEO was ousted in 1996, only three years after launching the revolution. The new CEO wisely returned to the focus on birds, but even so, Audubon has never recovered its peak membership of the late 1980s."

THE PROBLEM: SEEING THE FOREST THROUGH THE TREES

There is a lot of good sense in the traditional advice of defining a target audience, identifying their wants, and giving them what they want. However, a more complete picture is needed for organizations interested in ideologically transformative goals. When you focus on the ideology you are seeking to change rather than the individual, decision-maker or organization, you quickly notice your proxy audiences (i.e., those who influence your usual audience) become your primary audiences and you understand where your most important opposition comes from. When it comes to understanding your audience, the psychological characteristics of individuals or even groups, while important, will never be enough. To understand why people do what they do, you need to understand the social conventions, or systems of thought, that structure the world they inhabit.[150] This will in turn inform why certain things predictably make them feel the way your psychological research tells you they do. This will require you to understand those systems on their own terms instead of just through your critical lens (however valid it may be).

Defining Audience: Addressing the Silent Opposition

The main task of the innovating ideologist is to legitimate some behaviour previously viewed as questionable or to render questionable some previously accepted behaviour.[151]

The structure of how people think about things is not in the hands of any one decision-maker or group, although obviously some groups are more influential than others. Consequently, though narrowing your audience as much as possible is good advice, you should not narrow your audience to the point that you lose sight of the fact that

[150] Skinner, *Visions of Politics*, 90-91.
[151] Skinner, *Visions of Politics*, 148.

you are trying to change a system around the decision-maker and not just the decision-maker.

For example, let us say you favour a particularly expensive policy. The obvious first audience is the legislator at the level of government with authority over the policy. They tell you, however, explicitly or through their actions, there is simply no way the government can afford such a measure. The traditional advice at this point would be to appeal to key constituents, allies in the party and so on, all with the aim of applying pressure to that primary audience. If you can only apply enough pressure, they will find the money somehow. You successfully apply a great deal of popular and strategic pressure. However, all the government responds with are half-hearted pilots and vague promises about what they will do with the result. You come to realize that ideas about how and to what extent governments can raise financing for such policy mean that your proposal is in fact impossible under the current framework.

If Skinner was studying this question about why these legislators have such deeply entrenched ideas about government financing, he might start to look at the texts that likely shaped these decision-makers. Do they have similar educational backgrounds?[152] What did their business, political science, or law studies teach them?[153]

What are the influential think tanks associated with their party? Why do they think the way they do?

Follow this down the rabbit hole a few decades (or hundreds of years), as Skinner would do and what quickly becomes apparent is that when your goal is ideological transformation, you are trying to influence the ideological influencers. Your first audience may actually be a professor in a quiet hall somewhere rather than the decision-maker at the centre of the halls of power. More likely, it will be a constellation of authorities in different roles in the academy, civil society, the private sector, and government that all support and reinforce one another building the common words and ideas that form at least part of the ideological structure in which your target decision-maker operates.

[152] Quentin Skinner, *From Humanism to Hobbes.* (Cambridge: Cambridge University Press, 2018), 63-88.
[153] Josh Dehaas, "Election Analysis: Most Common Occupation for Candidates in Each Party," *CTV News*, October 9, 2015.

Studying your audience this way also makes it apparent why truly systemic change requires a longer view. The other thing that quickly becomes apparent is that your audience may primarily be made up of your ideological opponents, people who think differently from you.

Strategic communications advice already recognizes that your opponents are an important audience. However, your biggest ideological opponent is not the one who will cry out in protest against what you are calling for. The forces that have to show up to rally against you aren't nearly as powerful as the forces that don't. The most transformative ideas will likely provoke the least explicit resistance because, given the unlikelihood of acceptance, no one will feel the immediate need to oppose it. If there is a real justification gap that you need to fill, then it is the systems of ideological influencers that quietly feed your decision-makers' assumptions that are your true opponents. The wider the justification gap, the less individuals and organizations who sustain these assumptions will need to respond to you.

In saying that your opponents are your most important audience, I am not suggesting that you should abandon addressing your supporters and potential supporters. Rather, I am suggesting that in addressing your supporters and potential supporters, you are always also tacitly addressing your opponents. Your message will be able to make further inroads into how people think (and not just what people think) if you are selecting where and how to apply pressure based on the weak points in the current structures of thought.

As I will discuss later in this chapter's exercise, addressing your supporters and opposition simultaneously means crafting your arguments in a way that appeals to your supporters, but is also calculated to highlight the inner-contradictions and tensions of your silent opposition's moral vocabulary, while simultaneously offering a solution that members of the opposition are capable of adopting from within their own world view as a resolution to the dissonance they will feel. By addressing your supporters and opponents in this way, you will appeal to your supporters in the ordinary way but also force those among the opposition who see the contradiction to seek to change their moral vocabulary in a way that should bring it closer to what you need.

There is one major exception to the above line of thinking. If your goal is not to change current structures but exclusively to build up alternative structures, then it may be acceptable to address only your supporters on only their terms. However, to the extent that you will ever need to address external structures, developing some sense of who the silent opposition is will be strategically valuable. For example, religious communities that seek to isolate from broader North American society sometimes face major opposition from child welfare, law enforcement, and other established systems. It is very important for them to understand the inner logic of these systems to be able to deal with them even if only on a situation-by-situation basis.

You may also be concerned that this method will carry you too far away from your specific mission and therefore lead to mission drift. This is a valid concern but recall the case of the Northern Italian Cities who wanted to be independent of the Holy Roman Empire. Until the general barrier of how Roman law was interpreted was addressed, the individual city-states simply could not proceed with their claims of independence.[154] As long as you develop a precise theory of how your specific mission fits into the bigger picture, working on the bigger picture may cause mission drift in a superficial sense, but it may also prove to be a precondition of ever accomplishing your specific mission.

Understanding Your Target Audience: The Forest Not Just the Trees

Everything I said in Chapter 2 about understanding your ideological environment can also be used to understand key audiences you are targeting, their communications, and actions.[155] This approach focuses on the ideological environment of the audience rather than the individual characteristics of the audience members. This is crucial to understanding where they are coming from, but it is also key to keep your focus on the fact that you are trying to change the environment not just the individual. Understanding the emotion of your audience is of course helpful. The rhetoric Skinner studies is also fundamentally concerned with addressing the emotions of audiences.[156] But there is a risk of losing the forest of your audience in the trees within it.

---

[154] Skinner, *The Foundations of Modern Political Thought*, 65.

[155] Skinner, *Visions of Politics*, p.134, 140.

[156] Skinner, *From Humanism to Hobbes*, 222-315.

While studying individual characteristics will likely point you to patterns of thought within certain audiences, it does not explain the social meaning of those patterns. It may be interesting to know that a white, middle-class suburban mother is particularly anxious about crime, but without understanding the sense, reference, and attitude implicit in those words, you will not understand the true significance of that opinion. And you won't understand those words without the bigger structures of thought in which they exist.

Influencers identified above, such as important books, sources of media, traditions, and so on, are proxy audiences, and they need to be understood before you can understand your target audience. The social conventions form the backdrop against which individuals express their opinions.[157] Understanding these systems that influence your audience as they understand themselves is important. For example, if you were addressing people influenced by a religious tradition, you may need to have knowledge of the teachings, practices, doctrines, theology, and methods of that religion and the specific interpretations prevalent among your audience.

These proxy audiences are therefore not merely a means to influencing your audience, but a crucial starting point in understanding them.

When it comes to understanding decision-makers, understanding their personal characteristics, relationship to their constituents, and policy agendas is part of the frame. But so is understanding the backdrop of the movement or ideas in which they are embedded. The more you understand and adapt your strategy to the underlying thinking of the ideology of a particular party, for example, the more you will be able to exercise a consistent kind of persuasion on decision-makers despite their idiosyncrasies.

If we understand the war of words as being over this structure of how important decisions in society are made, then each particular decision may be considered a battle. It is quite possible to win a battle in a way that does not advance your overall cause at all. For instance, if your ideological goal is to ensure that workers receive better pay and working conditions because of their intrinsic value as humans, arguing that better pay leads to higher productivity gets you no closer

---

[157] Skinner, *From Humanism to Hobbes*, 142.

to workers being intrinsically valued, and in fact may set you back, to the extent that it is a view that likens workers to machines.

Skinner provides a brilliant example of this in the case study of Lord Bolingbroke's Parliamentary opposition to the government of Robert Walpole from 1726 to 1735. His opposition was based on such issues as the corruption of Parliamentarians and the existence of a standing army.[158]

At the time, the idea of the organized and concerted opposition that Bolingbroke led within Parliament was against constitutional conventions and viewed as immoral, if not outright treasonous.[159] Consequently, Skinner argues that Bolingbroke needed principles that were accepted and recognizable to justify his conduct to overcome the "obvious impermissibility" of his conduct. If the charge is treason, it stands to reason that the best defence is in fact patriotism, and because this was his defence, Skinner argues, it fundamentally shaped the type of government decisions Bolingbroke attacked.

Because the Whig ideology of his time (the name of the governing party and philosophy) had specific views about the need for balance between executive and legislative branches and the dangers that standing armies pose, Bolingbroke's opposition specifically attacked the executive's use of pensions and offices to gain support of Parliamentarians, as well as the large spending on a standing army.[160]

Before Skinner, theories about Bolingbroke were incapable of explaining precisely why he had chosen the method of attack he had chosen. Bolingbroke undoubtedly cleverly appealed to the emotions of the public and government officials. However, if we stopped the analysis there, it is not clear that we would be able to understand the full force and kind of accountability Bolingbroke was bringing to bear on the government.

It is not enough to understand a system from the perspective of its critics. You need to understand it the way it understands itself.

---

[158] Quentin Skinner, *Vision of Politics Volume II, Renaissance Virtues* (Cambridge: Cambridge University Press, 2002), 344-367.

[159] Skinner, *From Humanism to Hobbes*, 353.

[160] Skinner, *From Humanism to Hobbes*, 356-360.

The Danger of Giving the Customer What They Want

It is obviously true that when you communicate with someone, you should consider their needs. In giving people what they want, however, one always risks reinforcing the status quo, since people's current desires are shaped by it and, depending on the audience, likely reflect it. There are obvious examples of this, such as how adapting projects to meet funders' needs rather than community needs shifts control away from communities.[161] Subtler and more pervasive is the equivocation in much strategic communications advice between the audience's needs and wants, which are not the same thing.[162]

Most crucially, there appears to be an unspoken assumption that you can discover the already fully formed wants/needs of your audience by doing research. This assumption reflects a market-oriented understanding of individual wants as something that individuals form on their own and bring into the marketplace.[163] This assumption is reflected even among advisors who reject simply copying market approaches.

But if you cannot discover your audience's needs through research, how can you determine your audience's needs? According to Skinner and others, peoples' needs, and moral identities are formulated in the process of deliberation, rather than being discrete and pre-given before you meet them in dialogue.[164] It is therefore a positive development for strategic communications advisors to advocate for two-way dialogue. There is a big difference, however, between taking in information to better reflect it back to your audience so that you can ultimately get what you want and treating your strategic communications as a process by which you are working with the audience to reformulate both your and their understanding of their needs.

What are these needs that we discover through demographic and psychological research, among other techniques? The most plausible

---

[161] INCITE! The Revolution Will Not Be Funded, 9, 11, 14.

[162] Benjamin Miller, "Theorizing Legal Needs: Towards a Caring Legal System" (Thesis, University of Ottawa, 2016), 28-52.

[163] Deborah A. Stone, *Policy Paradox: The Art of Political Decision-Making.* (New York: W. W. Norton and Co Inc. 2012), 229.

[164] Stone, *Policy Paradox*, 229; Joan Tronto, *Caring Democracy: Markets, Equality and Justice* (New York: NYU Press), 17-45.

answer, it seems to me, is that they will reflect the assumptions of your current moment, which is to say the ideology you are trying to transform.

If your audience is constantly in a process of formulating and reformulating its needs, then one need your audience will always have is for help in this task. Indeed, even official decision-makers with an official party agenda are constantly in the process of formulating their needs. For example, they must decide how their agenda can best be implemented or applied to unforeseen circumstances, and they seek input from stakeholders they perceive as important to the decision.[165] If this is true of someone with a platform, how much truer is it of a member of the public?

Look at the National Audubon Society example and ask, "Do the expressed wants of our audience contradict our goal?" or "Is the customer always right?" If you exist for the sake of the members, then David Williams was right. Taking a much more aggressive approach to environmental issues in opposition to the members was a huge mistake and the decline in membership and fundraising was an unfortunate consequence. However, if you exist for the sake of the birds, or at least the ongoing appreciation of birds, then perhaps it was a tactical mistake to change too much, too fast. However, a decline in membership and donations is not in and of itself a bad result if remaining accountable to more members would necessarily mean not being able to pursue the range of strategies needed to protect birds. We could retell the story of the National Audubon Society as courageously becoming a leaner, more ideologically focused organization with the support of its members to take the bold actions necessary to help birds for generations to come.

If your organization is embedded in the community, it can provide structured and well facilitated opportunities for open conversation in that the community. However, you will not be able to understand the significance of the needs expressed to you until you have evaluated those needs in light of the broader ideological structure.

---

[165] Benjamin Miller, "Democratic Dialogue and the Political Art of Listening." *Half a Maven*, September 18, 2019.

THE SOLUTION: IDENTIFYING THE SILENT OPPOSITION

In this exercise, you will identify the key players who maintain the structures that you need to change or replace by identifying those actors who can most obviously deliver the change you want to see. You must then formulate their reasons for rejecting your proposal in similarly precise and succinct language to your justification for advancing your claim.

By comparing your justification to the reasons your desired action is rejected enables you to more precisely identify the ideological mismatch or shortcoming in your justification. Once you have done that, you will need to identify the sources of the objections. And the sources of the objection to your ideas will be your ultimate audiences and for whom engaging with those audience will be necessary for longer-term effect, although they may or may not be your direct audiences.

Step 1: Identify Immediate Decision-Makers

Identifying your silent opposition starts with identifying your "immediate decision-maker". The immediate decision-maker is the individual or organization who has direct control over the action you would like to legitimize or delegitimize in pursuit of your mission.

To identify your immediate decision-maker, ask:

- What is the activity I am trying to legitimize or delegitimize?
- Who does the action or would do the action?
- Are they an individual or an institution?
- Who has the power to stop the action from happening?
- Are they an individual or an institution?

Example: Bystander Intervention Approach to Gender-Based Violence

What is the activity I am trying to legitimize or delegitimize?	Delegitimize gender-based violence
Who does the action or would do the action?	Primarily men
Are they an individual or an institution?	Individual
Who has the power to stop the action from happening?	Those around the man committing the violence
Are they an individual or an institution?	Individuals (friends, family, colleagues, etc.)
	Institutions (workplaces, schools, public transit, etc.)

In complex modern societies, there will be a wide range of individuals and institutions involved in even the simplest action. Consider, for example, how many people and institutions are involved in eating breakfast. The identity of your immediate decision-maker, therefore, is more of a function of the specific point in the chain you have decided to focus on.

Step 2: Why the Immediate Actor Has Rejected Your Proposal

The next step is to determine why the decision-maker has so far done the thing you are seeking to delegitimize, writing it out the same way you wrote out your own justifications for your aims. They may have given a reason for their decision.

Individuals may provide you reasons for their decisions if you just ask. Even if it is not their true reason, it still represents what they believe is a sufficient justification to provide for their actions.

For public decision-makers there are a range of sources you can check:

- Government websites
- Comments to the press
- Election platforms and other party documents
- Hansard (transcripts from the legislature)
- Legislative committee reports and transcripts
- Budget notes and explanations

- Responses to reports by auditor-general, privacy commissioners, ombuds-people and like officials
- Academic articles in public policy, history, political science and related fields
- Interviewing people close to the decision or decision-maker
- Court cases
- Ask the decision-maker

If they have not given a public explanation, then you must reconstruct their justification. This is not a simple process. Skinner's method suggest you can reconstruct their justification by understanding the beliefs of the decision-maker about what they are doing. Assuming their rationality, we can work backwards by trying to explain how a given decision made sense in the context of that set of beliefs.[166]

This means you must understand three things:

- **What do they likely believe about their own role in the decision?** For example, how much discretion do they believe they have? What do they believe their goal should be in the situation?
- **What do they likely believe about the issue?**

What Does a Decision-Maker Believe About Their Role?

To understand a decision-maker's decision, it may be tempting to jump straight to their beliefs about the issue. But their beliefs may be a moot point if they believe their role requires them not to act on their personal beliefs. For example, a bystander may agree that it is wrong for one partner to demean and belittle another, yet also not believe it is their place to say anything.

There are cases where a decision maker's beliefs about their role in a situation make their beliefs in an issue totally moot. Take for example, the case of the Governor-General dissolving Parliament on the advice of the Prime Minister, or the Electoral College in the United States electing the President according to the candidate who received a plurality in their state. Although these decisions may once have been

---

[166] Tully, ed. *Meaning & Context*, 90-92.

discretionary,[167] these decisions no longer represent a judgment of the merits by the actors involved, but rather their belief that they are bound to abide by the constitutional conventions that govern their roles. Yet, they would not include this as an official rationale for their decision. You would need to know the history of these positions.

To understand what somebody might believe about their role, you can look at:

- Job description
- Legislation that sets out their powers
- Professional standards or constraints
- Speaking to other people who have had that role
- Speaking with the individual themselves or people close to them
- Textbooks or academic articles geared towards students preparing for that role

What Does a Decision-Maker Believe About the Issue?

In order to determine what a decision-maker likely believes about an issue, you should look at whether they have commented about it in the past or what they are likely to believe about an issue given their broader outlook. One interesting technique is reconstructing a decision-maker's justification by considering how the opposition framed its criticism of the decision, which the decision-maker has rejected.

Prime Minister Stephen Harper's decision to end the mandatory long-form census in 2010 provides a very interesting example in which beliefs about the decision-maker's role and issue both played a very prominent role.

The *Statistics Act* of 1971 states that "The Governor in Council shall, by order, prescribe the questions to be asked in any census taken by Statistics Canada…"[168] Between 1971 and 2009, this process went off without a hitch. Every five years, Statistics Canada would submit a list of proposed questions for the census to Cabinet, based on their

---

[167] The Canadian Encyclopedia, King-Byng Affair.
[168] Statistics Act (R.S.C., 1985, c. S-19) at sec. 21(1).

own wide consultation. There would be minor back and forth followed by approval.[169] Even though formal authority rested with the Cabinet, this process ran so smoothly that, until 2009, workers at Statistics Canada commonly considered it an independent agency.[170]

When Prime Minister Stephen Harper made the long-form census voluntary, the criticisms showed that many generations of decision-makers believed that approval would be a fait accompli. Academics, civil society, provincial and municipal governments, and industry reacted with almost universal disapproval.[171] They pointed to how useful and used this data was. The frame of the debate came from a couple of widely cited articles by scientists who argued that the content and methodology of the census is a scientific question, and the Conservative government's decision constituted an ideologically motivated encroachment on what should be autonomous scientific decision making.[172]

The justification the critics used to try to delegitimize the decision to end the mandatory long-form census could be summarized as follows:

"Government should continue to treat Statistics Canada as an independent agency in order to preserve the integrity of the scientific process, thereby ensuring the highest quality of data to academics, civil society, government, and industry so they can make evidence-based rather than ideology-based decisions."

---

[169] S. McDaniel, H. MacDonald, "To Know Ourselves – Not," *The Canadian Journal of Sociology/Cahiers Canadiens De Sociologie*, 37 No 3 (2012): 255; I Fellegi, "Statistics, public confidence and lessons from the story of the 2011 Canadian Census," (August 1, 2012): PPT, slide 4; Statistics Canada, *Guide to the Census of Population*, 2016. (Government of Canada, 2017): Chapter 4.

[170] McDaniel and MacDonald, "To Know Ourselves – Not", 256.

[171] M. Adams, "From compulsory to voluntary long-form census: What we stand to lose," (Ottawa: Policy Options, 2010); "Manitoba, Ontario among provinces backing long census." *CTV News*, July 20, 2010; Haroon Siddiqui, "Gutting of census stirs opposition to Stephen Harper," *Toronto Star*, July 10, 2010.

[172] M. Yeo, "The Rights of Science and the Rights of Politics: Lessons from the Long-form Census Controversy," *The Canadian Journal of Sociology/Cahiers canadiens de sociologie*, 37 No 3 (September 2012): 297, 302.

From this, you could then formulate the justification for taking a different course of action. In this case, the Minister responsible, Tony Clement, formulated the justification as follows: because those who do not fill out the census are threatened with fines and even jail time, "the legislation requires democratic accountability before the penal power of the state is engaged."[173]

You must then ask firstly why each party thinks the other's rebuttal is not sufficient. In this case, supporters of the mandatory long-form census argued that no one has ever been imprisoned,[174] although individuals had been fined.[175] The implicit rebuttal then seems to be "because the coercion is largely symbolic so too should the oversight be." The Government in this case must either be taken to believe that even "symbolic threats" require substantial democratic oversight or else it was not purely symbolic.

The Government's justification could therefore be summarized as follows:

> *"Decisions about the long-form census are democratic, not scientific, because the long-form census is backed by the threat of force. A voluntary census does not compromise the integrity of the scientific process, so academics, civil society, government, and industry can still have access to data."*

Step 3: Identify Who Has Influence Over That Justification

Once you have formulated the justification, you can start to identify the keywords and the institutions and actors that create the ideological structure that provide the particular sense, reference, and judgment value of these words. If you have limited time, try to identify the one most important driving factor in the decision and explore the ideological structure around that.

Identify sources by spirals starting from the decision-maker and going outwards:

---

[173] House of Commons, Standing Committee on Industry, Science and Technology. Minutes of Proceedings. 3rd Sess. 40th Parliament. (Government of Canada: July 27, 2010), Meeting No. 29.

[174] House of Commons, 40th Parliament. Meeting No. 29.

[175] *R v Finley*, 2013 SKCA 47 (CanLII http://canlii.ca/t/fxctz).

- Their staff, researchers, and actors responsible for informing their decision.
- The philosophy or position of their organization or political party.
- News coverage of the issue from periodicals they are likely to read.
- Opinion pieces from commentators they are likely to take seriously.
- Reports and books on the subject written from a point of view they are likely to endorse.

You can fill in this form to identify the silent opposition reinforcing the justification to refuse your position.

Sources of Ideological Support

Influential colleagues or advisors:

_____

Organizational context (e.g., manager/employer, political party):

_____

News (newspapers, podcasts, TV programs, radio shows):

_____

Journalistic opinions (editorials, magazines):

_____

Reports (government, think tank, trade association, nonprofit):

_____

Books (academic, popular, classic, contemporary):

_____

Social media influencers:

_____

Pay close attention to whether these sources are internally consistent and consistent with one another. For example, a source may emphasize the importance of government supporting businesses and also speak about the illegitimacy of state coercion. In the case of the long-form census, businesses spoke about how useful the data was to them. This therefore produced a tension within the structure that supports the decision-maker's justification. Noting these tensions will be crucial for future chapters.

Chapter 6

Not What You Say but How You Say It

So far, we've talked about mapping your linguistic environment, setting goals, planning, and identifying audiences and the arguments used to resist change. It's time to start thinking about crafting the actual message you are going to carry out to the world and how you are going to disseminate that message. In this chapter, we will briefly discuss the ideas of issue framing and reframing, as well as how to choose communications channels. I will then offer a catalogue of reframing tactics that Skinner observes and the way to categorize communications channels for the purposes of the 100-Year PR Plan.

In this chapter you will learn:

- How to prioritize which keywords to seek change in
- How to choose different change tactics to accomplish different purposes.

CONVENTIONAL WISDOM: FRAMING ISSUES AND CHOOSING CHANNELS

According to George Lakoff, a linguistics and cognitive science professor at the University of California, Berkeley, issue frames are "mental structures that shape the way we see the world."[176] The trouble for you is that an issue may not be framed in a way that encourages people to act on it or respond in the way you want.

To overcome this problem, your messages to the public need to "reframe" the issue. According to Patterson and Radtke, reframing is "the process of selecting pieces of information and organizing them to produce new perspectives in order to generate public engagement."[177]

Once you have figured out how your message will frame an issue, you then need to decide how to spread your message. When choosing between different mediums, received wisdom suggests you consider what channels:

- your target audience pays attention to.
- your relationship with your audience would make acceptable.
- will affect audiences in different ways.
- will allow you to control your message.
- can be effectively used given your skills.
- are within your budget.
- could be re-used to reach other audiences.[178]

There are a huge range of communications channels to choose from and you will almost certainly use a mix of them. Peter C. Brinckerhoff says that your communications material should also solve a problem for your audience.[179] This could be as old-school as sending out a calendar with key dates for a particular community or as advanced as developing an app your audience can use to figure out how to save energy.[180]

THE PROBLEM: SAME FACTS DIFFERENT LIGHT

There are two basic issues with the above. Firstly, it suggests that issue framing is about choosing different facts and rearranging facts. The

---

[176] Patterson and Radtke, Strategic Communications, 90.
[177] Patterson and Radtke, Strategic Communications, 91.
[178] Patterson and Radtke, Strategic Communications, 113.
[179] Brinckerhoff, *Mission-Based Marketing*.
[180] Kivi Leroux Miller, "27 Communications and Marketing Tactics for Nonprofits," (Nonprofit Marketing Guide, 2019).

heart of ideological change, however, is being able to redescribe the same facts. Secondly, the discussion of choices between mediums fails to distinguish between the two basic ways ideological change happens: you explicitly make the case for it and you implicitly make the case for it by using words in a novel way.

Rhetorical Redescription: Same Information Different Light

Reframing is not just about selecting information and organization to provoke a new reaction. This is one way to reframe an issue, but it is not the most basic way. The more fundamental reframe is taking the exact same information and casting it in a different light, often through the use of neighbourly terms. For example, two terms may be "neighbours" in that they can be used to describe the same set of facts but carry a very different judgment value.[181] For instance, you can call the same act "brave" or "rash", "funny" or "foolish", "memorable" or "scarring". Skinner calls this "rhetorical redescription" and it is at the heart of ideological change.

The expression "one man's freedom fighter is another man's terrorist" gets exactly at this point. The two people contemplated in this expression may disagree about the facts, but even if they agreed on the facts, they probably disagree at a much more fundamental level about whether it is ever acceptable to use violence to achieve political objectives.

In fact, the word "terrorist" originated during the French revolution to label supporters of the Jacobins who advocated for terror and violence as a means to achieve principles of democracy and equality.[182] Notice how the term has evolved from meaning exclusively a state policy to now most often referring only to non-state actions against the law.[183] Those who attempt to apply the term to state actions now generally use the label "*state* terrorism".[184]

---

[181] Skinner, *Visions of Politics*, 184.

[182] Online Etymology Dictionary, 2020, "terrorism" https://www.etymonline.com/word/terrorism.

[183] Alex P. Schmid, *The Routledge Handbook of Terrorism Research*. (New York: Routledge, 2011), 48.

[184] Anthony Aust, *Handbook of International Law, 2nd ed.* (Cambridge: Cambridge University Press, 2010), 265.

This is a clear example of a "reframed issue". Yet this transformation could not have come about simply through the strategic presentation of information. You could present the exact same set of violent actions and political objectives to someone. Whether they frame it as terrorism or not will crucially depend on whether they believe the term refers only to state actors, non-state actors, or is capable of referring to both.

This insight of Skinner's method is important particularly in our times when there is much concern that people do not share a common reference point for facts. It means that it is possible to reframe an issue even working exclusively with the set of alleged facts presented by the silent opposition.

Do What I Say or What I Do

When you seek to reframe an issue, therefore, you are often doing one of two things. You are taking the same information as your opponent and either:

1. explicitly making the argument that a certain label should (or should not) apply to it, or

2. simply using the label and therefore implicitly making the argument that it ought to apply.

For example, it is one thing to write an essay about how it is tyrannical for a government to limit access to barbershops owing to a health crisis, and another to have mass hair-cuttings outside the legislature with a sign that says, "end tyranny".[185] The audience may be persuaded by the essay if they find the arguments sound or the writing to be moving. How the protest manages to persuade is more difficult to capture, but involves such factors as:

- Who is attending? Will the decision-maker's decisions be affected by seeing those people concerned?

- How is the event talked about, particularly by those who maintain the ideological structures around the decision-maker?

- Are a lot of people going?

---

[185] Alex Abad-Santos, "How hair became a culture war in quarantine," *Vox*, June 10, 2020.

Skinner's studies center on great works of political theory, which of course fall into category one. But the events he looks at and the range of materials that shape the environment in which those great works largely come from category 2. These two categories provide you with a way to classify communications channels. Ideally, you can use most channels in either way though they will lend themselves to one or the other. For example, a protest sign is much better in category 2. A book or how-to-guide is much better in category 1.

THE SOLUTION: CRAFTING YOUR IDEOLOGICAL STYLE GUIDE

In Chapter 4's exercise, you articulated the justification for your position in the keywords. Ideally, you took notes about where the conventional sense, reference, and judgment value were inadequate to convey your argument. In Chapter 5's exercise, you identified the decision-maker's reasoning for rejecting your position (either failing to pursue an action you view as legitimate or engaging in an action you view as illegitimate). As part of that exercise, you identified what keywords are particularly important for the decision-maker, as well as the sources maintaining that structure.

It is now time to identify the specific ways you can aim to change keywords so that:

- Those keywords which fail to justify your position are better able to do so
- Those keywords that justify the status quo are less able to do so.

Think of these as part of your reframing analysis as you craft your messages.

You do not need to limit yourself to the way your justification is currently stated. In reading these tactics, you could realize there are other keywords that should be incorporated into your justification.

Step 1: Prioritizing What Words to Go After

As I have said previously, you should not be more innovative than you have to be. This is partly because you have limited resources, and partly because the more things you try to change at once, the less you will be able to benefit from the claim that your interpretation of a moral language is more coherent overall.

Firstly, look at the keywords that you identified in your justification and the keywords the decision-maker used in their justification. The keywords in these two places should be your general scope for words to focus on. Wherever there is overlap is a very good place to start.

Keywords in my justification for change   **Keywords in decision-maker's justification to reject**

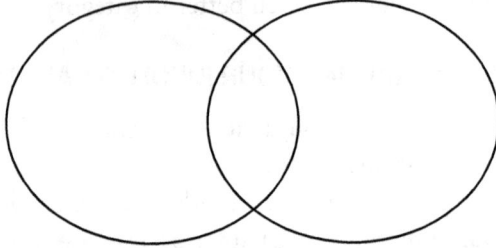

Secondly, consider in Chapter 2's exercise, you drew a word map. The lines you drew between words indicated which were structurally important words (i.e., a lot of other words depended on them). The colour for words you used indicated how contested their meanings were. The most difficult words to change will be words that are structurally important and settled. These will require truly long-term planning (for example first going after the words they depend on). The easiest words to change will be structurally unimportant and highly contested. The sweet spot is for words that are structurally important but contested.

Compass for Prioritizing What Words to Seek Change

Contested

These are keywords which may be useful as part of a broader strategy but should not distract you.	These are keywords ripe for immediate efforts at change.
Ignore these keywords.	These are keywords worth building up to for long-term change.

Structurally unimportant (left)   **Structurally important** (right)

Settled

How to use the compass:

1. Get some flip chart paper and draw a graph with four quadrants.

2. Label the top "contested" and the bottom "settled". Label the left-most point "structurally unimportant" and the right-most point "structurally important".

3. Write each keyword you will be considering on Post-it notes.

4. Based on your word map, place the Post-it notes on the graph.

   a. Pick a point at which you consider a word to be neither structurally important nor unimportant (e.g., 2 other words depend on it). That point is the "0" point. More than that is structurally important. Less than that is structurally unimportant. Use judgment.

   b. How settled a word is, is really a matter of judgment.

5. The more structurally important the farther to the right it goes. The more contested, the higher it goes.

Simultaneously, if your goal is for the current structures to come tumbling down, you are going to want to be building alternative structures. For this purpose, you will want to prioritize keywords that are settled and structurally important but re-purpose them. This will provide you with a solid foundation.

Step 2: Choosing the Right Tactics for the Job

Once you have identified which keywords you will work on, you can begin to create an ideological "style guide". In this style guide, based on the tactics you choose below, you will set out what sense, reference, and judgment value each word will have. This way, everyone in your organization can refer to the guide and know what they can use the word for, and in what range of situations, in all your communications.

There are various ways you can change keywords to reconfigure the existing structure or undermine it to build a new one. Recall that all terms have a sense (their definition), reference (the range of cases they apply to), and judgment value (the implicit attitudes the word evokes in the audience). Each tactic below will involve using a word in a way that changes at least one of these three aspects while keeping 1-2 of the others constant.

Below I will go through the main tactics that Skinner has observed, as well as some I have added. Some of the tactics can be used only to strengthen a word you need for your justification or weaken a word the current justification depends on. Many can be used for either purpose. For each tactic, I will examine it in its legitimizing form (i.e., legitimizing a condemned activity) and delegitimizing form (undermining an accepted activity).

To choose the tactic right for you, think about:

- Which aspect of the word is holding it back from assisting your justification?
- Which aspect is most heavily contested and therefore most ripe for change?
- Which aspect does the decision-maker depend on in order to be able to use it to justify their disagreement with your position?

Tactic 1 (Positive): Capturing Good Terms

Sense	Reference	Judgment value
De-emphasize or eliminate parts	Expand	Maintain

You may use a positive word in your justification to support an activity others condemn. Skinner points out that words like this can be made broader to include the activity you are interested in legitimizing by de-emphasizing some part of the word's sense.[186] This is sometimes done by insisting that the essence of the word is really that part that does apply to the activity you are trying to legitimize, and the other aspects of the definition are secondary or optional.

Examples of this strategy include:

- The use of the word "love" to describe same-sex relationships, as in "it shouldn't matter who you love" to counter a

---

[186] Skinner, *Visions of Politics*, 149.

NOT WHAT YOU SAY BUT HOW YOU SAY IT

previous tacit exclusion of same-sex relationships from this term, or else to take the focus off of it by focusing instead on "sexuality" whose emotional impact on audiences is much more mixed than love (i.e., it evokes both positive and negative attitudes depending on the audience). "Love" as a concept plays a central role in Christianity and therefore may have had a strategic appeal to certain oppositional demographics.[187] Notably, the success of this strategy has been observed to be context specific.[188]

- The term "free speech" to describe what others might call "hate speech" to both bring it within legally protected speech and to align its propagation with a historically counter-authoritarian movement. This expansion of the reference implicitly removes certain qualifications in the definition of the term "free speech" thus altering its sense. The free speech movement was aligned with the civil rights movements of the 60s, and therefore may have resonated with individuals who historically opposed racist and sexist speech.

- The term "triple bottom line" expands the reference of a term of high priority to businesses by de-emphasizing aspects of the sense which restrict it to specifically monetary value.

There are also risks to expanding terms to include increasingly more activities. For example, to legitimize housing supports for a wider range of people, "homelessness" in Canada now includes precarious and insufficiently housed individuals, whereas before it did not.[189] However, as a result a single term is used to refer to various situations which may require different interventions, so that it then requires further distinction to which many audience members may be insensitive.

The fact that you must insist on some part of the meaning as being so present in your case that it justifies de-emphasizing the other parts

---

[187] Skinner, *Visions of Politics*, 169-70.

[188] Joy L. Chia, "'What's Love Got to Do with It?': LGBTQ Rights and Patriotism in Xi's China" *Australian Journal of Asian Law*, 20 No. 1, (November 21, 2019).

[189] Canadian Definition of Homelessness, *Canadian Observatory on Homelessness*, 1. https://www.homelesshub.ca/sites/default/files/COHhomelessdefinition.pdf.

will necessarily result in you reproducing the existing structure, at least in part. In fact, if you are strategic about which positive term you use in your justification, you can benefit from not only the force of those words but the ways of thinking they represent.[190]

Examples of integrating the behaviour within an entire system of thinking include:

- The term "social enterprise" and the use of the term "entrepreneur" in government and non-profit contexts integrate and thereby justify a range of policies and programs by embedding them within market-oriented thinking.

- The term "artist" to describe someone who does "graffiti" which was meant to elevate the practice and integrate it with other visual arts.

- The term "profession" used to mean joining a religious order before it shifted in meaning being practiced in work one professes to be skilled in.

Tactic 1 (Negative): Depriving Opponents of Good Terms

The reverse of each of these tactics is also possible. You can deprive an existing activity of a positive description by narrowing the definition of that positive term (i.e., narrow the reference by adding to the sense). Examples of this include:

- Insisting that true adherents of an ideology believe X.

- The environmental movement by strategic use of the word "cost" have sought to undermine the claim that goods are "cheap" by describing environmental impacts as hidden costs.

You can also strategically use terms to align a practice with broader structures of terms that are condemned. Examples of this include:

- Referring to protests as "riots" may align them with "crime", which is condemned as a class of activity.

- Protesters frequently use swastikas on signs to align the thing they are protesting with Nazism.

However, beware. If you change the meaning of a word too much it

---

[190] Canadian Definition of Homelessness, *Canadian Observatory on Homelessness*, 151.

may simply lose its force and undermine the point of the transformation in the first place.[191]

Tactic 2 (Positive): "Owning" Terms with Negative Connotations

Sense	Reference	Attitude
Maintain	Maintain	Reverse/Vary

Quentin Skinner defines the tactic of what is colloquially called "taking back" a word, as using a term in such a way as to make clear to your ideological opponents that what they consider a bad term you are using positively (or at least not negatively).[192] This is a useful tactic when part of the decision-maker's justification is a condemnation using pejorative terms for what you are trying to legitimize.

Some examples of this include:

- When Justin Trudeau committed to deficit spending as a way to signal his party's progressiveness in the 2015 election, it broke at least a decade-long taboo around the word/practices of "deficit spending".[193]

- The Canadian extremist group Proud Boys describes themselves as "Western-chauvinists" using a term that was coined as an insult for excessive and blind loyalty to Napoleon nearly 200 years ago,[194] and has been used in various insulting ways since.[195]

- The "Slow" Movement is built around a word that in modern North American society is generally viewed negatively and turning it into an ideal (e.g., slow food).[196]

---

[191] Skinner, *Visions of Politics,* 168.

[192] Skinner, *Visions of Politics*, 152.

[193] Campbell Clark, "Trudeau Betting Most Canadians Don't Care About Deficits," *The Globe and Mail*, March 24, 2016.

[194] Online Etymology Dictionary "Chauvinism" https://www.etymonline.com/word/chauvinism.

[195] Southern Poverty Law Center (2020) "Proud Boys" https://www.splcenter.org/fighting-hate/extremist-files/group/proud-boys.

[196] www.slowmovement.com.

Tactic 2 (Negative): Disowning a "Good" Term

The reverse of tactic 2 can be practiced in two ways, one far more common than the other. The first is taking a positive term that is used by the decision-maker to justify some course of action you are seeking to delegitimize and using it with negative connotations. Common examples of this which Skinner himself points to include "chivalrous" or "gentlemanly".[197] Since this is an obvious and widespread tactic, I will not go into more detail.

The less obvious way to practice this tactic is to take positive terms ascribed to one's own group or movement or activity and "disown" them (i.e., by systematically excluding them from your justifications). There are many examples of groups discarding stereotypes, such as "hard working" as a way to legitimize exploitative labour practices, or "sensitive" as a way to discount one's ability to reason. Similarly, many involved in poverty relief have moved away from describing their work as "altruistic" as it undermines their professional character.[198] This is a reflection of the fact that ideological structures always come with constraints. One cannot mobilize their legitimizing force without also in part being directed by them.

Tactics 1 and 2 can be mirrored by expanding the application of a negative term to include something you want to delegitimize or narrowing it to exclude something you want to legitimize. For example, many previously accepted behaviours in the workplace would now be widely considered harassment or assault. Similarly, the term "victimless crime" has been used to try to narrow the condemning force of the label "crime" to those illegal activities with a clear or obvious victim.

Tactic 3 (Positive/Negative): Coining New Terms

After looking through all these tactics, you may find that the existing moral vocabulary is simply incapable of justifying your ultimate goal. In that case, you may need to come up with new keywords either by inventing words or combining terms to create totally new concepts.

---

[197] Skinner, *Visions of Politics*, 169-170.
[198] Dan Pallotta, "The Way We Think About Charity is All Wrong." TED2013, March 2013.

Although Skinner calls this a "crude device" and observes it less frequently than other strategies,[199] there is no question that coining new terms is a tactic that can be mobilized both to legitimize and delegitimize certain behaviours, identities, movements, and policies. As previously discussed, when we examined the P2P Foundation accounting report, this strategy is still heavily used by some. Particularly successful examples of this in recent years include:

- "Ecological/environmental/carbon footprint" which has been successful both at identifying a thing to be condemned and also providing a methodology to measure it, thus enabling its reduction.[200]

- "calling out/calling in" which legitimizes a way of policing shared space that might otherwise be viewed as impolite.[201]

- "racism" was also only coined in 1936 and its impact cannot be overstated.[202]

Tactic 4 (Positive/Negative): Extending Neutral Terms

Sense	Reference	Attitude
Expand by metaphor	Expand	Make positive or negative

While I have mainly focused your attention on keywords that have evaluative and descriptive aspects, Skinner also points out that writers often mobilize neutral terms by expanding their meaning through the use of metaphor.[203] This can be a great way to seize real estate that no one will fight you for or expect and can be used either to legitimize or delegitimize a group, behaviour, or movement. For instance, "census" could hardly be said to have been a particularly sensitive word in Canada until 2010 when it became the fault line of a significant ideological disagreement.

---

[199] Skinner, *Visions of Politics*, Volume, 151.

[200] "Ecological Footprint: Overview". footprintnetwork.org.

[201] Sian Ferguson, "Calling In: A Quick Guide on When and How," *Everyday Feminist,* January 17, 2015.

[202] Rob Kyff, "20 Most Important Neologisms of Century," *The Hartford Courant,* December 8, 1999.

[203] Skinner, *Visions of Politics*, 151-152.

One interesting example of this tactic is the use of historical figures. The names of individuals can have significant rhetorical value, as we have seen recently with regard to debates over public statues, for example, those of John A. MacDonald.[204] Those controversies are obviously over figures whose names already have some evaluative weight one way or the other. However, reassessing and mobilizing historical figures who have otherwise been largely forgotten by the public can be useful.

Quentin Skinner discusses how throughout the Medieval period, the philosophers Cato and Cicero were largely viewed as Stoic sages aloof from politics; however, when republicanism was popularized through the translation of the works of Aristotle, they were reappraised as patriots and shrewd public officials who defended liberty.[205] Note for instance that Cato's name was borrowed for the name of the influential American think tank, the Cato Institute.

Examples of contemporary terms that start with neutral terms, expand them through metaphor, and use the expanded term to either legitimize or delegitimize include:

- "Customer" which though neutral has been used through metaphorical extension to expand the application of market thinking to many non-market domains.

- "Leak" which though having the connotation that something is wrong physically had no significant political connotation, has since been applied to information to condemn its distribution to the public.

- "Manufacture" and "engineering" were both relatively neutral terms that were extended through the use of metaphor to "manufactured consensus" and "social engineering" to condemnatory terms (i.e., because in being applied to people they imply the treatment equates people to objects).

---

[204] Bernie M. Farber, David B. MacDonald, Michael Dan, "Should Statues of John A MacDonald be removed?" *Toronto Star*, August 21, 2018.
[205] Skinner, *The Foundations of Modern Political Thought*, 54.

Tactic 5 (Positive/Negative): Watering Down Terms

Sense	Reference	Attitude
Maintain	Expand	Neutralize

This is a tactic exclusively geared towards denying the decision-maker some word they rely on to justify their current disagreement with your desired course. Similar to the "taking back a word" tactic, this tactic operates through the repeated use of a word in situations other than its prevalent usage. In contrast, however, you are not trying to win over the word to your side but neutralize it or water it down.[206] This may also happen over time within a movement when a word used to legitimize or delegitimize an activity is used so often it begins to lose its weight.[207]

Although I have not found any textual evidence of this, a knowledgeable friend once told me that some alt-right groups online insist on using certain slurs as often as possible and in such a range of contexts in which they are meaningless so that listeners and readers will become totally desensitized to them, and therefore not understand the opposition to them.

Tactic 6 (Positive/Negative): Boycotting Terms

One simple way Skinner points out to rob a word of its force that the decision-maker may rely on is simply to use it less frequently.[208] As it is used less frequently it will often lose its potency. Additionally, consistent with what Skinner observed above about how a single word can bring a whole way of thinking into the argument, I would add the exercise of finding alternatives to certain words is a way of displacing the structures of thought the replaced words represent.

Obviously, you would have to be a pretty big organization for your refusal alone to use a word to make any significant dent. But even if you are a smaller organization, by including in your style guide never to use certain words, you are forcing your staff and volunteers to find

---

[206] Skinner, *Visions of Politics*, 152.
[207] Skinner, *Visions of Politics*, 153.
[208] Skinner, *Visions of Politics*, 169-70.

other ways to get a message across, and you may propagate alternative ways of speaking that will catch on and replace it more broadly.

This is not quite the same thing as stigmatizing the use of a term (e.g., a slur). Stigmatizing the use of a term often increases its potency (i.e., by adding shock value and increasing the attention paid to it) but delegitimizes the speaker. Boycotting a term is more about making a term disappear quietly through disuse.

Tactic 7 (Positive/Negative): Insisting You Are Only Using a Word Descriptively

Sense	Reference	Attitude
Maintain	Maintain	Neutralize

Another strategy to deny the force of a term that the decision-maker depends on is to explicitly say you are using a word neutrally that would normally imply a certain judgment.[209] He offers the examples of "culture" or "civilization".

Step 3: Choosing Your Communications Channels

Once you have created your style guide, you should then determine what communications channels you will use to spread these changes. There are two types of communications that spread linguistic changes.

1. **Tools that help you explicitly make the case for the linguistic innovation.** These tools include publishing a book, report, manifesto, lecture, class, holding a conference, or some other usually long-format medium.

2. **Tools that implicitly spread the linguistic innovation by using it.** These tools include basically any communications in which you use the keyword creatively, in such a way that your meaning is clear. For example, a protest sign that says "Meat is Murder" redefines murder without making the case for it.

In order to accomplish the transformation both will probably be necessary. However, if someone has already written a book that makes the case for the transformation you have identified as needed, then you

---

[209] Skinner, *Visions of Politics*, 169-70.

will choose those channels that help spread and translate their work for the audiences you have identified as key. On the other hand, if no one has written that work yet, you may need to engage in some intellectual heavy lifting or work with others who can compose the kind of long-format content that will serve as an intellectual foundation from which you can draw in your shorter communications.

Whether or not someone else has written the book, it is always worthwhile to help spread the change through repeated use in attractive ways that will help expressions catch on.

Chapter 7

There is No Marketplace of Ideas

This chapter examines conventional wisdom on competition in the nonprofit sector and its limitations when applied to ideologically transformative communications. Increased competition is treated as a basic fact of life for a modern nonprofit. We will explore in some detail current methodologies for competitive analysis and collaboration. Even though I will ultimately propose an alternative, these methodologies are important to understand in some detail because the method I will propose will follow a similar structure.

We will explore the ways in which a market-based understanding of competition doesn't work for ideological innovation move away from competitive thinking and, in particular, focus on the "systems change" approach to philanthropy. At the end of the chapter, I will share a Skinnerian method for an "ideological competition" exercise that focuses more on identifying your allies.

In this chapter you will learn:

- Why there is no marketplace of ideas
- How to identify potential allies
- How to identify ideological competitors.

CONVENTIONAL WISDOM: GETTING AHEAD IN THE MARKET

Much communications advice views competition as a basic fact of nonprofit life arising out of the increasing number of nonprofits competing over limited resources. While there are different views on whether this competition is a good thing, most accept it as inevitable. Therefore, advisors recommend analyzing your competition using competitive analysis techniques.

The Necessity of Responding to Competition

There is a consensus that increased competition is a reality for contemporary nonprofits,[210] derived from the idea there are more nonprofits than ever before, and they are competing for funds, employees, volunteers, and marketing opportunities.[211]

The competition makes it difficult to cut through what's called "the white noise", "the background noise", and the "clutter".[212] Faced with this noise, your ultimate goal, they say, is to beat your competition in order to further your mission.[213]

Competition is also actively encouraged by a number of important actors in the nonprofit sector. Governments who have adopted a market-oriented mindset favour competition among funding applicants.[214] Charity ratings agencies encourage it by publicly comparing organizations.[215] Crowd-funding platforms encourage it by increasing the number of organizations donors can easily reach and learn

---

[210] Melanie Randle, Friedrich Leisch and Sara Dolnicar, "Competition or collaboration? The effect of non-profit brand image on volunteer recruitment strategy," *Journal of Brand Management*, 20 No. 8 (September 2013): 689.

[211] Kinzey, *Promoting nonprofit organizations*, 23; Wiggill, *Strategic communication management*, 227; Peter Frumkin and Suzi Sosa, "Competitive Positioning: Why Knowing Your Competition Is Essential to Social Impact Success," *Non-profit Quarterly* (March 20, 2018).

[212] Kinzey, *Promoting nonprofit organizations*, 18; Patterson and Radtke, *Strategic Communication*, xiii; Williams, *Marketing & Communications*, 7.

[213] Brinckerhoff, *Mission-Based Marketing*, 24.

[214] Terri Kline Henley, Donald Self, Walter W. Wymer, Jr., Marketing Communications for *Local Nonprofit Organizations: Targets and Tools* (New York: Routledge, 2011), 24.

[215] Amanda Wright, Challenges In Achieving Non-Profit Sustainability: A Study Of the Social Service Non-Profit Sector In The Central Okanagan (Scotiabank Centre for Non-Profit Excellence 2015), 9.

about.[216] Furthermore, "customers" encourage competition, since nonprofits compete to remain in the good graces of their customer.[217]

According to this history of the sector, up to a point, some not-for-profits enjoyed monopolies.[218] David Ongenaert observes that "Since the 1980s, the number of organizations in the humanitarian landscape has increased significantly. This has led to a fierce competition..."[219]

Is Competition a Good Thing?

Many commentators say that competition is a good thing because it encourages efficiency and better-quality service.[220] Furthermore, it is a way to make sure that society's limited resources are not wasted on organizations that will squander them.[221]

Others say that what is increased efficiency is just anxious territorialism in the nonprofit sector.[222] This is because where for-profits can improve their products and expect others to come back, there is no guarantee that a donor or funder has been attracted to another organization because of the quality of the nonprofit's services. Rather, it could be that they have simply re-prioritized different causes. Consequently, nonprofit professionals worry that they simply will not be able to help those they aim to serve.

Others say competition is bad because it forces organizations to promote what they have done whether or not it was actually successful.[223] As a result, nonprofits do not share their failures and learn from their collective experience.

[216] Wright, 9.

[217] Brinckerhoff, *Mission-based marketing*, 23.

[218] Spencer Creal, "Why Competition in the Nonprofit Sector is Frustrating," Nonprofit Hub (November 15, 2017).

[219] David Ongenaert, "Refugee Organizations," 195–206.

[220] Teri Kline Henley, Walter W. Wymer, Donald Self Jr, *Marketing Communications for Local Nonprofit Organizations: Targets and Tools* (New York: Routledge), 2011.

[221] Otis Fulton and Katrina VanHuss, "Sizing Up Your Nonprofit Competition," *NonprofitPro*.

[222] Creal, "Why Competition in the Nonprofit Sector is Frustrating?"

[223] INCITE!, *The Revolution Will Not Be Funded*, 10.

Competitive Analysis: Identify and Evaluate Your Competition

Whether or not competition is good or bad, advisors agree it is here to stay, so the next step is to advise you how to understand your place in it and how you should respond to it.

Many advisors recommend that you do a competitive analysis not only once but on a regular basis.[224] Some recommend that you use existing competitive analysis methods such as SWOT or the Six Forces Model.[225]

Whatever method you use, there are two basic steps to a competitive analysis. Firstly, you identify the competition. Secondly, you compare yourself to them according to a given set of criteria. By comparing yourself to other similar organizations in your field, it often immediately signals the magnitude of your proposed innovation.[226] It will also highlight where you are strong and where you can improve.

Warning: Below I will explain the steps of a conventional competitive analysis in some detail, so you understand its logic and process. Although, ultimately, I will propose an alternative to this method, it will be helpful for you to understand the conventional method, because my proposal will mirror it.

Step 1: Identifying Your Competition

Advisors have different ways of defining who you are in competition with. Often, they use the term "market" to differentiate between competitors. Peter Frumkin, a nonprofit leadership scholar at the University of Pennsylvania, and Suzi Sosa, a social entrepreneur in leadership training, define a market as "summation of the various providers offering the same product or service, usually within a finite set bound by a specific customer or geography."[227] They say your competitors are those who share your: geography, clients, or services/products. Those who offer the same product/service are those most important competitors.

---

[224] Frumkin and Sosa, "Competitive Positioning".
[225] Frumkin and Sosa, "Competitive Positioning".
[226] Frumkin and Sosa, "Competitive Positioning".
[227] Frumkin and Sosa, "Competitive Positioning".

Teri Kline Henley, a nonprofit communications scholar at Loyola University, describes the difference between direct and indirect competitors.[228] Direct competitors are other organizations in a similar area with a similar mission. Indirect competitors are organizations with a different mission who are ultimately competing for the same dollars. Otis Fulton and Katrina VanHuss, volunteer and fundraising consultants, break indirect competitors into those that meet the same need in a different way, and those that do not compete for clients but do compete for other resources.[229] You can also divide up competitors over what you are competing over, such as money, staff, volunteers, clients.[230]

If you cannot identify any direct competitors, this probably means you are encountering risk and[231] will want to determine why no one else has entered the market, or, if they have, why they did not last.

One of the advantages of identifying your potential competition is that you can also identify your potential collaborators.[232] A potential collaborator is an organization that complements your offerings without having too much overlap with you.

According to this method, you should gather basic facts about your competition such as: What services do they provide? What clients are they seeking? What value do they give to the customer? What are their prices?[233]

Step 2: Compare Yourself to Your Most Direct Competitors.

Once you have identified a group of 10-20 competitors, narrow it down to 5-7 most direct competitors.[234] This narrower list of groups will most closely resemble your most important characteristics and will help you answer:[235]

---

[228] Henley, Wymer, Self, *Marketing Communications*, 123.
[229] Fulton and VanHuss, "Sizing Up Your Nonprofit Competition".
[230] Brinckerhoff, *Mission-based marketing*, 121.
[231] Frumkin and Sosa, "Competitive Positioning".
[232] Frumkin and Sosa, "Competitive Positioning".
[233] Brinckerhoff, *Mission-based marketing*, 130.
[234] Frumkin and Sosa, "Competitive Analysis".
[235] Frumkin and Sosa, "Competitive Analysis".

1. What characteristics describe your organization but not your competitors?

2. What characteristics describe your competitors but not your organization?

3. Which of these answers matter?

There is no science to choosing the characteristics to use as the basis of your comparison. Frumkin and Sosa, quoted above, recommend starting with those characteristics that you feel distinguish your organization. These characteristics could be internal, such as the quality of your product or service, or they could be external, like your relationships or location.

Once you have a list of all the characteristics you feel you possess, you can look at whether any other organizations surpass you on any or all of these.[236]

Differentiate Yourself in Response to Competition

Once you understand your competition, advisors then recommend you differentiate yourself from them. This may take the form of a "position statement", which is a statement that emphasizes why you are unique.[237] In fact, according to some, the main purpose of communications in a competitive world is to define and defend your position, emphasizing why you are unique.[238]

Differentiating yourself is not just the main recommendation of communications advisors, but also what scholars have found nonprofits actually do in a competitive environment.[239] Interestingly, once they distinguish themselves, they then set up a hierarchy of values that puts whatever makes them unique on top of what distinguishes their competitors.[240] For instance, Amanda Ashton, Editor of Change Better, a publication for nonprofits, recommends that when appealing to donors or funders, you focus on your competitive

---

[236] Brinckerhoff, *Mission-based marketing*, 125.

[237] Upleaf Technology Solutions, "Nonprofit communications plan template".

[238] Williams, *Marketing & Communications*, 2.

[239] Emily Barman, "Asserting difference: The strategic response of nonprofit organizations to competition." *Social Forces*, 80 No 4 (2002): 1192.

[240] Barman, "Asserting difference," 1195.

advantage either by differentiating your services or emphasizing that you can do something at a lower cost.[241]

Don't Beat 'Em, Join 'Em (With Systems Change)

Even advisors and scholars that advocate for the value of a competitive analysis also strongly encourage collaboration.[242] Although this collaboration is generally with organizations you are not competing against. This kind of collaboration can be an organization's competitive advantage.[243] Put simply this is because "there's no reason to go it alone when you can place your message in other people's mouths."[244] For example, David Williams, the nonprofit communications scholar mentioned earlier in the book, points to AARP as an example of a savvy organization that is successful because it knows the political coalition it needs to build and targets those partnerships.[245] Collaboration is also encouraged by industry experts who see it as a method of more effective service delivery.[246]

It's not simply that partnership can be helpful in getting your message across. Rather, it can be necessary in order to reach people who otherwise would not listen to you. Williams points to the partnership between nonprofits seeking to reduce teen pregnancies and television producers of teen dramas. A strong case can be made that because the producers included narratives of teen pregnancies that emphasized the social drawbacks, teen pregnancy then declined considerably.[247] Similarly, collaboration might be necessary because the problem is so large that no single organization can tackle it alone.[248]

Some observe that it is particularly important to get your potential opposition onside. For example, The Pew Foundation specifically targeted religious organizations it believed would oppose its

---

[241] Amanda Ashton, "Competitive Analysis: Why your nonprofit needs to size-up the competition change better," *Medium* (December 3, 2018).

[242] Randle, Leisch, Dolnicar, "Competition or collaboration?", 1.

[243] Frumkin and Sosa, "Competitive Positioning".

[244] MissionBox Staff, Drafting a Nonprofit Communications Strategy, April 1, 2020.

[245] Williams, *Marketing & Communications*, 10.

[246] Wright, "Challenges in achieving non-profit sustainability", 10.

[247] Williams, *Marketing & Communications*, 12.

[248] John Kania and Mark Kramer, "Collective Impact" *Stanford Social Innovation Review* (Winter 2011).

population control efforts, and successfully recruited many of them, thus nullifying much of their opposition.[249]

Of the many collaboration methodologies, I will discuss the recent example of "systems change", also called "collective impact". "Collective impact works on a sharing of knowledge and resources to address specific needs within a community."[250] Systems change focuses on leveraging the existing organizations and networks to solve problems too big for any single organization to solve.[251]

Systems entrepreneurs bring together like-minded organizations to focus on a common problem, marshaling the unique resources of each organization.[252] One way dozens of organizations can be focused on the same thing is through developing a common set of metrics.[253] Often it is the funder who plays the role of curator and steward of organizations around an issue.[254]

There is not much consideration of the possibility that if you are not doing anything meaningfully different from your peers, you may not need to be a separate entity at all.

THE PROBLEM: THERE IS NO MARKETPLACE OF IDEAS

In this section, I will assess whether the above understanding of nonprofit competition is appropriate for understanding ideological competition. I hope to convey four main ideas. Firstly, a market-based understanding of competition is fundamentally inappropriate for ideological competition. There is no marketplace of ideas. Secondly, you should see those who are most similar to you as your allies not your competitors, even if they are competing for resources. Thirdly, when it comes to comparing yourself to your competition, ideological innovations must be judged according to how useful they are. Finally, I will argue that successful innovation is not about emphasizing your uniqueness but offering innovations that resonate with existing ways

[249] INCITE!, *The Revolution Will Not Be Funded*, 13.
[250] Wright, "Challenges in achieving non-profit sustainability," 10.
[251] Jeffrey C. Walker, "Solving the World's Biggest Problems: Better Philanthropy Through Systems Change," *Stanford Social Innovation Review* (April 5, 2017).
[252] Walker, "Solving the World's Biggest Problems".
[253] Kania, Kramer, "Collective Impact".
[254] Walker, "Solving the World's Biggest Problems".

of thinking. These innovations must be useful to others not involved in your issue in order to succeed.

Ideological Competition is Not Market Competition

A market-oriented understanding of competition is inappropriate for nonprofits interested in ideological transformation for two main reasons.

Firstly, ideological competition is not a recent phenomenon in the nonprofit sector. As long as nonprofits are trying to fill a justification gap it means that there is silent opposition in the existing structures that have prevented the nonprofit's mission from being achieved. Nonprofits may have once had a monopoly over fundraising or service provision in a geographical area, but they have clearly never had a monopoly over the means by which social problems are created or solved, and these are of course the most important kinds of competition for a nonprofit's mission.

Secondly, the market understanding of competition starts from assuming the scarcity of resources, but legitimacy is not a scarce resource that can be acquired like funds or staff.

A market approach to understanding ideological competition puts the emphasis on finite resources. But, as we've discussed, the "resource" involved in an ideological competition is legitimacy. Legitimacy is not acquired so much as shaped.

What is the difference between saying public support is acquired versus shaped?

If support could be owned, we would assume that a person could wield it to the exclusion of others. But you simply cannot build a fence around public support no matter how much you try to keep other people out.[255]

A single organization working on an issue creates an empathy for that issue other organizations can benefit from. Most people can use most words as part of their efforts to advance their cause. Moral vocabularies are also non-exclusive in the sense that others can make

---

[255] You can of course make it much more difficult for other people to spread linguistic change, for example, by monopolizing access to communications technology, discouraging literacy, and other similar tactics. In this respect, an analogy with land is apt as people always do manage to slip through fences.

use of the language, benefitting from them, and also changing them through their use.

It may be that some people have greater credibility when they use certain words. When someone who has actually experienced a genocide invokes the term "genocide" it may carry more weight. Similarly, when someone considered an expert uses a technical term within their field, it may carry more weight than if someone else used it. For instance, when a medical professional calls something a pandemic it has a different weight from a non-medical professional doing so.

Yet, in practice, a wide range of people make comparisons to genocides and throw around technical terms. Moral vocabulary cannot be possessed.

This non-exclusive and pliable quality of moral vocabulary means that even the most successful ideological innovator can never seize the meaning of a word like they can seize property. Ideological competition is simply not a marketplace of ideas.

Competition is Neither Good Nor Bad

According to Skinner, ideological contest is simply something that is always going on.[256] It is therefore inappropriate to say whether it is good or bad. However, Skinner does give us some reason for thinking that more transparent ideological competition is a positive development. We should be wary about imagining some "good old days" in which there was allegedly consensus. Part of Skinner's historical project is to show us that alternatives to current dominant ways of thinking have always been there and should continue to push us to do better.[257]

Ideological Competitive Analysis

Even though I said a market-oriented approach to ideological competition is misleading, a competitive analysis is still a useful exercise and in this chapter's exercise, I will propose how it could be done to better suit ideological competition as Skinner sees it. Therefore, to prepare for the coming exercise, in this subsection, we will examine

---

[256] Tully, ed., *Meaning & Context*, 23.
[257] Skinner, *Liberty before Liberalism*.

what Skinner's findings, in contrast to the conventional wisdom, can tell us about who the real competition is, how to compare yourself to competitors, and whether your goal should really be to appear as unique as possible.

Identifying Your Real Competition

Competitive analyses suggested by advisors push you to think of those most similar to you as your most direct competitors. But if they are truly most similar to you, then in theory they should have similar interests in ideological innovations. That means that you should be able to present your 100-year PR plan to these similar organizations and invite them to join you.

Furthermore, because linguistic innovation is often most effective when it is not specifically tied to any organization but simply a part of the language (think "Pride", "Black", etc.), it will be easier for organizations to get past the concern that someone else will get the credit for their work. You simply cannot make change alone. You need many others to be pulling in the same direction with you and it helps both for the purpose of legitimacy and sustainability if they are independent from you.

Who, Then, is Your Real Competition?

In Chapter 5, we discussed how your real competition is the silent opposition in the existing structures of power. This insight is totally obscured when you focus exclusively on other service providers similar to you. However, the silent opposition is not your only relevant competition. Other organizations and actors inside or outside your "market" may be reinforcing the existing language or innovating at cross-purposes.

For example, ideologically speaking, refugee settlement organizations are not primarily competing among each other but against populist movements that deny refugees should even be allowed to enter the country.[258] Populist movements are also engaged in ideological innovation. Notice that they are not competing over finite resources such as funds or volunteers. If anything, they are trying to deny the access of funds for certain purposes to anyone. It could be

---

[258] Ongenaert, "Refugee Organizations," 196.

argued that they compete for the limited attention span of the public. While that is true, it misses the point. Fundamentally, these competitors are vying for the understanding and support of the public.

Those in your market who are using keywords differently may be your most direct competition. For example, one environmental organization may emphasize that it is possible to both grow the economy and protect the environment, whereas another emphasizes a post-growth economy. These nonprofits are ideological competitors even if they do not compete in any other way.

Ranking Your Competition: How to Judge Between Ideological Innovations

It makes sense that advisors recommend you come up with a list of criteria you believe are salient for your audience to judge between your services/products and those of your competitors. This will allow you to see where you stand vis-a-vis your competitors, and where your competitive advantages are. However, ideological innovations do not at first glance seem to be the same kind of thing as your products and services. How then can you compare your innovations to others on offer? Is there any way we can judge ideological innovations that would make a competitive analysis possible?

We've already discussed how a market metaphor is not appropriate because legitimacy is not a finite resource. Nevertheless, according to James Tully, Skinner does see words fundamentally as tools, and ideological innovation as a "service" rendered to some actor(s) in a political struggle.[259] As I have said many times before, ultimately, the goal is to advance an ideological innovation that helps legitimize or delegitimize some form of action. Consequently, you will want to compare your innovation to others based on how well the innovation does this.

Rather than asking, "what will my customer consider important when deciding what product to purchase?" you may ask "what will cause others to use these words the way I am proposing?". For example, in Chapter 4, I pointed out that one of the rationales behind the campaign to use "African-American" as a term was that it would help make claims for resources similar to those made by other ethnic groups. We could therefore expect (although I do not know) that it

---

[259] Tully, ed., *Meaning & Context*, 16, 23-24.

would be especially taken up by other organizations interested in making those types of claims.

The more people your innovation is useful to, and the more pressing and serious the problem it helps them solve, the more likely your innovation will be successful, even if those people have nothing to do with your issue directly. I will discuss why this is more below.

In addition to being useful, an ideological innovation must be sufficiently easy to use. In Chapter 4, I pointed out that coining new words is "costly" for the audience because it will be more difficult for them to integrate the new word into their vocabulary than it would be for them to use a word they already know differently.

While an innovation needs to be useful and usable, it does not need to be true. If an innovation is useful enough, it will succeed *even if everyone knows it is patently false.*[260]

---

[260] People are pretty cynical about politics, so I imagine it does not shock you to hear that according to Skinner's view politics has no necessary relationship to truth. What I think people appreciate less is that this seemingly amoral or immoral feature of politics is actually a function of its most democratic potential. This is because politics, particularly democratic politics, is fundamentally concerned with reconciling competing visions of what terms should govern our shared life (i.e., the space and resources we hold in common). A decision is not made because the facts support it but because the relevant actors support it. Because people are at odds about the truth, the decision-maker cannot simultaneously maintain a fidelity to the truth and to the claim all the actors make on them. Consequently, at its best, the indifference of politics to truth is a manifestation of its ultimate concern for the intrinsic importance of people in deciding the terms by which they should live together. That is not to say that politics has nothing to do with truth. There are two senses in which truth may impress itself on the political process. Firstly, obviously decision-makers may run up against reality sooner or later if their decisions are predicated on falsehoods (e.g., a bridge everybody wanted built quickly may collapse). Such confrontations with reality will definitely have an impact on the decision-makers going forward. However, what that impact is will be filtered again through the agnostic contest of competing ideas about shared life. Secondly, political actors may champion truth as a value relevant to shared life. However, it should be noted that all but the most cynical manipulating political operatives assume they are championing truth. Consequently, this is not very helpful. I take the time to make this lengthy comment because while Skinner's method is meant to be descriptive, I'm sure he would be the first to admit that the description shapes what he is describing. You may therefore justifiably ask whether it is ethical to buy into this vision of politics. Furthermore, I think there is an inherent risk in becoming cynical about the political process. My hope therefore in this note is to clarify that there is a way to accept Skinner's point about falsehood in politics without needing to be cynical.

Skinner provides the following example.[261]

During the English Civil War in the 17th century, the Whigs advocated for limits on the powers of the King. The Whigs claimed that the King's powers had been restricted by customary law since time immemorial. This version of history, however, had to confront the awkward fact of the Norman invasion in 1066 that could be said to have interrupted those restrictions on the king's power. The Whigs responded by denying that an invasion had ever occurred. This totally conflicted with what all the historians took for granted at that time as true. However, Skinner argues their claim was assured success, because it appealed to "every shade of opinion". Parliamentarians accepted it because they rejected absolute authority. Royalists could not reject it because they could not accept the legitimacy of conquest (since this would force them to recognize usurpers of the Throne).

For better or worse, useful fictions continue to play a central role in our lives. Perhaps the most famous, and one Skinner writes a lot about, is the existence of the state as a person.[262] Treating corporations as if they were their own legal persons capable of having the rights and obligations of a person is another pervasive fiction that implicitly every nonprofit corporation has bought into.

One caution, however. Besides the moral cost of propagating false-hoods, one of the costs of relying on fictions is that it may force you to question or deny the type of evidence that proves your claim is false.[263] So for example, the Flat Earth Society could never just be about whether the Earth is flat but would almost necessarily become opposed to the entire scientific establishment.

Think of who you need in your coalition and ask yourself whether your proposed ideological innovation will be useful to them to accomplish their goals. I will also discuss below how you want to think far beyond people involved in your immediate issue and ask yourself "how could anyone use this word?". You are building a tool and releasing it into the world. If you are not careful it can do a lot of

---

[261] Quentin Skinner, *Visions of Politics, Volume 3, Hobbes and Civil Science*, (Cambridge: University of Cambridge, 2002), 240.

[262] Skinner, *From Humanism to Hobbes*.

[263] Skinner, *From Humanism to Hobbes*.

harm, but if you design it well, then it will generally be able to help do constructive things.

Echo Existing Ways of Thinking

In this subsection, I will discuss how Skinner observed two things as crucial to the success of any ideological innovation. Firstly, if it echoes or resonates with existing schools of thought, it will benefit from existing institutions and networks because they will be more likely to start using the innovation. Secondly, the innovation must not only be useful in your own struggle but to many other similar struggles.

Do Not be More Innovative Than You Have to be

In earlier chapters, I stressed that you should not be more innovative than you have to be. This is because the more you can plausibly insist you are preserving the existing moral vocabulary, the more you will benefit from people's allegiance to that vocabulary. Here, I want to make a further point that your innovation does not have to be original. I know that does not sound very inspiring, but others have innovated before you. You should look at existing ways of thinking to see if anyone has innovated in the way you need (i.e., they have altered a keyword according to a tactic identified in Chapter 6's exercise). By echoing their innovation, you will likely benefit from their support.

Lutheranism spread rapidly throughout Germany, then through Denmark to Scandinavia, then through England and eventually to Scotland. Skinner argues that this can be explained by the already long-standing theological traditions that existed in those places since the Middle Ages.[264] These schools of thought, such as the Ockhamists and the Brethren of the Common Life, shared crucial theological ideas with Luther as well as what they thought these theological ideas meant in practice for the Church. Consequently, when Lutheranism emerged, the exponents of these already established schools tended to be pulled into the movement and strengthened it. Lutheranism therefore benefited from existing networks and institutions, such as universities where those traditions flourished, to spread its message.[265]

---

[264] Skinner, *Forerunners of Lutheranism*, 21-22.
[265] Skinner, *Forerunners of Lutheranism*, 21-22.

In addition to resonating with a school of thought, you can also try to appeal to the aesthetic of existing movements. For example, fascists in the 20th century took much of their aesthetics, such as marches and rallies, from the workers' movements of the time.[266] This was no accident. It reflected the fact that these movements were trying to appeal to the disenfranchised people who were ready for a significant change in one way or another. Essentially, these movements poached the followers of existing movements.

Your innovation does not have to resonate with a school of thought or movement. It could also resonate with a profession.[267] For example, in the early 20th century, the progressive education movement was quickly accepted by many school teachers and principals.[268] There are many reasons for this, but commentators include among them the fact that the progressive education movement valued their work and spoke to the problems they faced on a day to day basis such as decrepit buildings.[269] The language that the progressive school movement proposed provided these teachers and principals with the linguistic tools they needed to systematically articulate their problems and propose solutions.

Proponents of systems change philanthropy point to Education Superhighway as a success story. Formed in 2012, its goal was to upgrade the internet in every classroom in America. It wound down in August 2020 because it accomplished its goal. What accounts for its success? It quickly received millions in funding from the foundations of tech billionaires and was able to connect schools with this funding.[270] Their focus on improving education through technology no doubt immediately resonated with funders who were committed to the positive potential of technology. This is therefore arguably another example of appealing to a profession.

---

[266] Jacques Ranciere, *The Politics of Aesthetics* (London: Bloomsbury), 74.

[267] Skinner, *Visions of Politics*, 32.

[268] Sharon McKenzie Stevens, Patricia M. Malesh: "Active Voices Composing a Rhetoric for Social Movements," (State University of New York, 2009), 101.

[269] Stevens, Malesh, 101.

[270] About Us Education Superhighway. https://www.educationsuperhighway.org/about/.

The Dangers of Resonating with Existing Ways of Thinking

Ultimately, you must also be cautious about making your arguments palatable to existing ways of thinking. In the refugee settlement field, for example, humanitarian organizations have attempted to justify refugee acceptance in terms of states' larger economic and security objectives.[271] This has both gained traction with states but also limited what they are willing to do when refugee acceptance cannot be justified in terms of those objectives. This should not surprise us. As I mentioned in Chapter 2, ideology both enables by legitimating, but it is also always constrained by limiting legitimacy to the terms of that ideology.

The Ripple Effect of Ideological Innovation

In Chapter 2, we also discussed how moral vocabularies are connected. If you change the meaning of a word for the purpose of advancing your issue it may have many unforeseen ripple effects on other issues. If advocates involved in different issues take up your innovation, it will help to reinforce and entrench your success.

Alcoholics Anonymous (AA) is an excellent example of this. AA's famous 12 step plan was a codification of the principles of a mid-20th century Christian movement called the Oxford Group.[272]

Since then, AA has served as a model for many other types of mutual aid groups,[273] including Narcotics Anonymous, Clutterers Anonymous, and Sex and Love Addicts Anonymous, to name just a few. In some ways, the range of behaviours that addiction has come to describe and AA's relationship to the concept of addiction are classic examples of the ripple effects Skinner theorizes. AA's 12 step plan and model has also been applied to other types of issues, including racism, "under-earning", and survival of incest.[274] These other organizations may be totally independent of AA and work on completely different issues, yet they help to cement AA's place in society both as

---

[271] Ongenaert, "Refugee Organizations," 198.

[272] Alcoholics Anonymous, "Historical Data: The Birth of AA and its Growth in the US and Canada".

[273] Robin Room, "Alcoholics Anonymous as a Social Movement". (Toronto: Addiction Research Foundation, 1995).

[274] Underearnersanonymous.org, siawso.org.

an organization and a philosophy.

The interconnected nature of moral vocabularies has three big implications for your communications. Care needs to be taken that the changes you decided on in the last chapter do not negatively affect other issues you care about. You never just want to focus on the meaning of a word for your issue, but the role that world plays in upholding complete social philosophies.[275]

Your innovations can also be useful to others. Consequently, individuals and groups who at first glance have nothing to do with your issue can become strong allies because they have a stake in your innovation succeeding. In fact, according to Skinner's theory, uptake of your innovation by others not immediately involved in your struggle may be essential to your success.

James Tully, a major commentator on Skinner, put it as follows "... it is not necessarily or normally the immediate political struggle, but rather the circulation and adaptation of an ideology in the stratagems of a wide range of similar struggles that accounts for ideological entrenchment and hegemony."[276] There are a lot of five-dollar words there, but the basic point is you need to make sure your innovation will be a useful weapon in other people's fights too. In the case of Alcoholics Anonymous, the concept of anonymity and the 12 step plans proved very useful for others experiencing problems with much stigma attached to them.

Thirdly, the corollary to the above insight is that you will be at odds with anyone who prefers the current moral vocabulary to the innovated version. You therefore may find push back from unexpected places.

Systems Change and Ideological Competition

So, where does all this leave systems change? In one way, Skinner's insights support the push of systems change to leverage existing systems rather than try to build new institutions. However, the systems change methodology focuses on actively creating formal networks of collaboration to pool efforts under a single idea. Skinner is describing

---

[275] Underearnersanonymous.org, siawso.org, 165.
[276] Tully ed., *Meaning & Context.*

ideological resonances that are so strong there is no need for a formal relationship in order for everyone to pull in the same direction.

This difference is important for two reasons. Firstly, the examples of systems change philanthropy held out by its proponents all involve organizations who can provide millions of dollars in funding in order to facilitate and cement relationships between their fundees and other funders.[277] You may not have millions of dollars. Echoing existing ways of thinking provides an intrinsic reason for others to work together that does not depend on your access to significant funding or ability to coordinate other people on an ongoing basis.

Secondly, as we discussed in Chapter 3, there are significant issues that arise when movements are highly centralized and directed by funders rather than the communities being served. The coalitions Skinner describes remained fairly decentralized and fluid while still maintaining an ideological center before eventually solidifying. For example, many of the humanists who initially supported Lutheranism because they shared Luther's disgust of corruption in the Church eventually disavowed Lutheranism completely.[278] Furthermore, as I discussed above, to be successful, it is not enough to just have your own movement. Your innovations must serve others as well. It is simply not feasible in most cases for such a range of activities to be so centrally funded.[279]

THE SOLUTION: A COMPETITIVE ANALYSIS FOR IDEOLOGY

In this exercise, I will bring together the insights above by suggesting how you could do a competitive analysis geared towards ideological competition. Like a regular competitive analysis, it has two steps: identifying the competition and comparing your innovation against a subset of your competition. The main difference in the first step will be that your competition is those different from you rather than similar to you. The main difference in the second step is you will judge

---

[277] Walker, "Solving the World's Biggest Problems".

[278] Skinner, *Visions of Politics*, 27.

[279] The Koch Brothers in the States may be a rare exception to this. See Jane Mayer, *Dark Money: The Secret History of the Billionaires Behind the Rise of the Radical Right*, (New York: Anchor Books, 2017).

your innovation according to how useful and usable it is by others in your field *and in other fields.*

Step 1: Identifying Ideological Competitors and Allies

The first step is to identify ideological competitors and potential allies. There is no need to limit yourself to 10-20 organizations as advisors recommend. You are not just looking in the nonprofit sector, but in government, the media, the academy, and the private sector. Furthermore, you are not just looking at organizations, but individuals too, such as writers or filmmakers. Consequently, you may find dozens if not hundreds of relevant competitors. I recommend limiting yourself to 40 organizations with a maximum of 10 in any one sector. I suspect this will give you a fairly good sample of the range of voices out there. Note that you can probably use the research you did back in Chapter 2 and 5's exercise for generating this list.

You can identify competitors based on whether they are communicating about the issue you are interested in, especially if they are using the keywords you are interested in. However, even if they are not using the keywords you are interested in, they may still be competitors. Remember, the choice not to use a word, especially if everyone else in the field is using it, is an innovative strategy on its own.

Like in a traditional competitive analysis, you are most interested in other organizations and individuals addressing your audience. Depending how geographically specific your issue is, you may also limit your search according to geography. However, ideological innovation, unlike service provision, is seldom restricted to a catchment area.

Once you have identified your competition, you should divide them up into those who are using the keywords you are interested in:

1. In an innovative way similar to your approach

2. In a conventional way

3. In an innovative way at cross-purposes with your approach.

Obviously, the organizations and individuals in group number 1 are potential allies. This is true even if they compete with you in other ways. Among the organizations and individuals in groups 2 and 3, you should ask yourself whether they are intentionally at cross-purposes with you or just haven't thought about it. If you think someone just hasn't thought about it, you should consider approaching them. If you think they are genuinely at cross-purposes with you, then these are your genuine competition.

Competitor Identification List

Sector	Organization or Individual	Is their goal similar?	What keywords seem important to them?	Innovation similar, innovation different, conventional?	Strong Competitor (1) or Strong Ally (5)? (1-5)
Nonprofit					
Business					
Government					
Academia					
Media					
Art					

Step 2: Judging Between Ideological Innovations

Of the 40 organizations or individuals above, identify 5 organizations who seem to be your leading competitors per keyword you are interested in analyzing. There can of course be overlap, you are comparing how they use the word. Make sure in every group of competitors you have at least one who uses the keyword in a conventional way.

For each keyword create an ideological analysis comparative advantage spreadsheet.

1. Identify the organizations/individuals for whom that keyword is especially important and who you identified as being in competition with you (i.e., they use the word conventionally or are innovating differently from you).

2. Try to capture the sense, reference, and judgment involved in each competitor's use of the keyword.

3. Record how their sense, reference, and judgment value is distinct from the conventional use (e.g., wider-narrower, positive-negative, neutral).

4. Identify which tactic among those in Chapter 6's exercise they are using. You only need to put one example of an organization using each tactic in the spreadsheet.

5. For each innovative approach (as well as the status quo), you will want to ask:

   a. Who is this word useful to?

   b. How important is that use?

   c. How usable is it?

Always start the spreadsheet with an example of an organization or individual using a keyword in the conventional sense, because this will be your main competitor and you must judge the usefulness of your innovation against how useful the status quo is (and to whom).

Ideological Innovation Comparative Advantage Spreadsheet

Keyword: Insert Keyword Name

Organization or individual	Conventional or innovative	Sense	How sense differs	Reference	How reference differs	Judgment value	How judgment value differs	Tactic	Who does it help?	How important is the use for them?	How easy is it to use?
ORG 1	Conventional										
YOU	Innovative										
ORG 2	Innovative										
ORG 3	Innovative										
ORG 4											

The above analysis can obviously be quite time consuming, so if you do not have the time or resources, here is an example of a more fluid approach to analyzing competition over a keyword.

Let us consider the word "empowerment" since it is used for many purposes in the nonprofit sector. A quick Google search reveals a few things. Firstly, the dictionary at the top defines empowerment as follows:

- Authority or power given to someone to do something.

- The process of becoming stronger and more confident, especially in controlling one's life and claiming one's rights.[280]

We can observe two things about these definitions. Firstly, the examples make plain that the dictionary definition assumes a focus on the individual. This relates to the reference of the word (i.e., the range of cases it applies to). Secondly, we can already observe a tension between a formal grant of authority and a feeling. This relates to the sense of the word. The above definition is in stark contrast to its origins in community psychology, which emphasized both individual and communal autonomy and self-determination.[281] For example, Robert Adams defines it as

"Empowerment: the capacity of individuals, groups and/ or communities to take control of their circumstances, exercise power and achieve their own goals, and the process by which, individually and collectively, they are able to help themselves and others to maximize the quality of their lives." [282]

Secondly, when we look at the top search results, we see that it is mainly business media discussing the empowerment of employees. These articles use "empowerment" to express both an individual

---

[280] "Empowerment" Lexico (2020) https://www.lexico.com/en/definition/empowerment.

[281] Julian Rappaport, "In praise of paradox. A social policy of empowerment over prevention," *American Journal of Community Psychology*, 9 No 1 (1981): 13.

[282] Robert Adams, *Empowerment, participation and social work.* (New York: Palgrave Macmillan, 2008), xvi.

feeling and the delegation of tasks and decision-making author-ity.[283] Notice the subtle shift from both the dictionary definition and certainly the original definition. Authority is delegated to employees at the discretion of managers. The ultimate authority remains with the manager (and really further up the chain if we press the question). The employees' collective self-determination does not increase (although their operational autonomy may).

Furthermore, employee empowerment is consistently justified by these articles primarily in terms of increased productivity and second-arily in terms of happiness of employees. This alters the normative force of the word and connection to other words. This too is in stark contrast to its normative force in social work, where the empower-ment is for the sake of those being empowered. Interestingly, however, even its proponents in the business world acknowledge that most American employees do not feel empowered.[284]

We can pretty easily see from even the quick review above the insti-tutional structures behind these competing definitions. The Harvard Business Review and Forbes articles were written by academics. The Smarp article was written by consultants citing the Harvard Business Review. The community psychology definition was also written by academics but in psychology and social work. We start to have a sense of the actors and institutions invested in certain definitions.

Let us therefore ask the three questions assuming both groups are targeting employees.

[283] Allan Lee, Sara Willis, Amy Wei Tian, "When Empowering Employees Works, and When It Doesn't," *Harvard Business Review* (March 2, 2018); Joseph Folkman, "The 6 Key Secrets to Increasing Empowerment in Your Team," *Forbes* (March 2, 2017); Smarp, "Empowerment in the Workplace: Definition & Best Practices." (December 19, 2019).
[284] Smarp, "Empowerment in the Workplace".

	Business approach	Social work approach
Who is the word useful to?	Primarily the owners of businesses and managers who want to increase productivity, as well possibly consultants who may be hired to do it. Secondarily, employees.	Primarily the employees. Secondarily social workers who may be hired to increase empowerment.
How important is its use?	It promises to accomplish a fundamental goal (productivity). However, there are other business models that can do this.	Helps increase "autonomy". Whether this is viewed as important by the audience depends on how they view their current situation.
How usable is it?	Easily recognized because it connects to a common word (power).	Easily recognized because it connects to a common word (power).

Obviously, such an analysis can become much more nuanced and complex. My purpose in doing the above illustration is to show you can start to glean interesting insights almost immediately. In a full analysis, I would also look at how the word is used in other sectors.

So, once you have asked the questions, how can you use the insights to discover your competitive advantage? Even from the quick example above we can notice that employers are largely not heeding the call to "empower" employees and that employees are reporting serious dissatisfaction. This demonstrates a gap that is likely to make a definition of empowerment geared more directly at the employees rather than the managers more successful. This is a competitive advantage.

Identifying Schools of Thought You Can Draw on

As I discussed in the previous section, you also want to identify organizations and individuals who are not working on your issue but who are using the keywords you are interested in. You want to look at whether they are using the keywords in ways that could be useful to you. Finally, you want to find out the broader school of thought or institutional structure that use comes from. You may want to officially reach out to these organizations to, for example, say how you were inspired by them. This will give them an opportunity to take note of what you are doing.

Chapter 8

Social Media Changes Nothing

"The eye shall not be sated from seeing, nor shall the ear be filled from hearing. What has been is what will be, and what has been done is what will be done, and there is nothing new under the sun."

— Ecclesiastes 1:8-9

Social media platforms have largely displaced more traditional means of communicating such as newspapers. It is difficult to see how a nonprofit could hope to successfully engage in long-term ideological transformation without succeeding on these platforms.[285] *The 100-Year PR Plan* is based on insights Quentin Skinner developed by studying the Renaissance and Reformation in Medieval and early modern Europe. As you may know, they did not have Facebook. In fact, they did not even have Myspace.

You may, therefore, be forgiven for wondering to what extent those insights can be applied to communicating on social media. If they do apply, do they need to be changed? In this chapter, I will argue

---

[285] Kinzey, *Promoting nonprofits*, 25.

the answer is no. I will consider this question by focusing on some of the ways that social media communications may differ from the traditional mediums Skinner studied (e.g., books, pamphlets, speeches, etc.). I will show that Skinner's methods offer interesting explanations of why some online content succeeds. The exercise in this chapter will be to create a Skinnerian social media plan.

I have chosen to focus on the distinctive features of social media because the more general advice given to nonprofits about, for example, goal setting and audience targeting, is basically the same advice we have already looked at.[286] Consequently, I assume that everything said in previous chapters applies to online communications unless there is some reason to think online communications is different. In this chapter, therefore, I will try to determine whether social media is different in some way that would render *The 100-Year PR Plan* inapplicable. Nevertheless, for more basic practical guidance about social media, I recommend *Social Media for Social Good* by Heather Mansfield and *The Networked Nonprofit* by Beth Kanter and Allison H. Fine.

Two caveats before beginning. Firstly, I will be talking about social media in general. There are of course many social media platforms and they affect communications differently.[287] I am by no means an expert in all the different kinds of social media platforms. Generally speaking, I have in mind the major platforms including Facebook, Twitter, LinkedIn, Tumblr, Pinterest, Reddit, as well as Wikis, including Wikipedia and WikiHow. For the most part, I will speak generally and rely on you to use your judgment to determine which platforms a point may not apply to. Where I speak about one platform, it may simply be as an illustration or because that insight applies especially

---

[286] e.g., Here's another example of conventional advice: Adam Weinger's, "4 Strategies to Nonprofit Social Media Marketing" at https://www.nonprofitpro.com/post/4-strategies-to-nonprofit-social-media-marketing/ or Stacey Wonder's "4 Easy Steps to Develop a Social Media Content Strategy for Your Nonprofit" at https://trust.guidestar.org/4-easy-steps-to-develop-a-social-media-content-strategy-for-your-nonprofit.

[287] F. Comunello, S. Mulargia, L. Parisi, "The 'Proper' Way to Spread Ideas through Social Media: Exploring the Affordances and Constraints of Different Social Media Platforms as Perceived by Italian Activists," *The Sociological Review*, 64 No 3 (2016): 515-516.

strongly to that platform. For the most part, however, I will avoid getting into platform specific tactics that are best discussed by experts in those platforms.

Secondly, Skinner's methods are properly applied by looking at general trends over the long-term. I do not think social media has been around long enough to conclusively say it is categorically different or the same. This chapter, therefore, more than those before it, is meant only to be suggestive of how Skinner's insights could apply to ideological innovation on social media.

In this chapter you will learn:

- How to analyze images and videos rhetorically
- What features of a social media campaign make it attractive to traditional media
- Why Wikipedia and online education platforms are so important for you.

CONVENTIONAL WISDOM: SOCIAL MEDIA IS DIFFERENT

There are two basic ways to look at social media. Some look at it as a totally new thing that follows its own rules. Some look at it as being like offline networks and communications, just in a new package. Below, we are going to consider some of the things that might make it different. Firstly, it integrates multiple forms of media in ways that were not possible before. Secondly, it is interactive in ways that were not possible before. Thirdly, it is possible to produce and distribute content at a speed that was not possible before. Finally, the success of content is dependent on the central decision-making of a few mammoth organizations who set the algorithms of their platforms.

Social Media is Multimedia

The first thing that appears to make social media different from heavily language-based mediums of the past (e.g., books, pamphlets, newspapers, magazines, radio), is the range of audio/visual media it allows for. Social media allows you to share much more than just text. You can share images, videos, infographics, polls, music, and video games[288] to name just a few. There are also many multimedia formats, such as memes, which incorporate both images and text. Advisors consistently tell you to update your social media channels with visual and video content.[289] Nonverbal communication helps to more effectively relay your ideas.[290] Similar to text content, this multimedia content must affect the audience emotionally.[291]

Some say you will be most likely to succeed when you integrate different forms of media.[292] For example, some advisors recommend using memes.[293] Other advisors are more hesitant if the memes are not high quality.[294] But the bottom line is that social media is visual and if you want to succeed you have to figure out how to communicate visually.

Social Media is Interactive

The main distinctive feature of social media is that it is social (i.e., interactive).[295] Some scholars argue that it leads to a shallow form of connection that does not lead to meaningful action or lasting change.[296] Some have called this "slacktivism". Nevertheless, the interactivity of it is unavoidable. Interactivity means a few things for you practically. Firstly, it means that you can and should produce content

---

[288] See for example PETA's parody version of Pokémon available at https://games.peta. org/pokemon-black-and-white-parody/.

[289] Mission Box Staff, "Drafting a Nonprofit Communications Strategy"; Julia Campbell, "Steps to a Successful Nonprofit Social Media Strategy," *The Balance* SMB (July 16, 2019).

[290] Kinzey, *Promoting nonprofit organizations*, 155.

[291] Kayleigh Alexandra, "5 Examples Of Nonprofit Social Media Strategies (And What You Can Learn From Them)," *Wild Apricot* (November 7, 2019).

[292] Claire Azelrad, "The 9 Signs of a Successful Social Media Strategy for Nonprofits", Neal Schaffer (2017).

[293] Social Media Group. "Going Social: Tapping into Social Media for Nonprofit Success," Convio Services Team, (2010), 17.

[294] Beth Kanter, "Can Memes for Good Work for your Nonprofit's Content Strategy? Not on Facebook!" (September 6, 2013).

[295] Kinzey, *Promoting nonprofit organizations*, 144; "Social Media Group, Going Social," 10.

[296] Jonathan A. Obar, Paul Zube, Clifford Lampe, "Advocacy 2.0: An Analysis of How Advocacy Groups in the United States Perceive and Use Social Media as Tools for Facilitating Civic Engagement and Collective Action" *Journal of Information Policy*, Penn State University Press Vol. 2 (2012): 2.

that allows others to participate. Secondly, it means that your content can and should reference other people's content. Thirdly, it means that you have to use the slang and norms of the online community that forms. Finally, it means you have to give up some control over your content as it is used by others.

Firstly, advisors tell you your content is more likely to succeed if you give your audience something to do.[297] Asking questions is a simple way to engage audiences.[298] It is also possible organize events online, such as "Twitterstorms" in which large groups of people organically create a lot of buzz and attract the attention of more traditional media.[299] This interactivity should empower your supporters to influence the conversation.[300] You should also not be shy to participate in conversations on the pages and groups of other organizations relevant to you.[301]

Secondly, social media gives you an increased ability to respond to and reference the work of others and share their content.[302] This allows for organic conversation and exchanges of ideas to happen. Nevertheless, even on platforms that highly encourage sharing, many advisors focus mainly on your own created content.[303] To know who to reference takes ongoing "listening" to your environment through setting up Google alerts, joining the right groups and following the right individuals.[304] This will also allow you to determine where your

---

[297] Kinzey, *Promoting nonprofits*, 153; Elise Dopson, "Social Media for Nonprofits: How to Make an Impact with Little Budget" (Sendible, 2018).

[298] Kevan Lee, "Social Media for Non-Profits: High-Impact Tips and the Best Free Tools," Buffer (n.d).

[299] Comunello, Mulargia, Parisi, "The 'Proper' Way to Spread Ideas through Social Media," 517.

[300] Social Media Group, "Going Social", 6.

[301] Kevan Lee, "Social Media for Non-Profits".

[302] Kinzey, *Promoting nonprofit organizations*, 52.

[303] Kinzey, *Promoting nonprofit organizations*, 161; David Chapman; Katrina Miller-Stevens; John C. Morris; Brendan O'Hallarn, "Social Media as a Tool for Nonprofit Advocacy and Civic Engagement: A Case Study of Blue Star Families," *Social Media and Networking*, (Hershey, PA., IGI Global), 66 – 93; Hugo Asencio, Rui Sun, *Cases on Strategic Social Media Utilization in the Nonprofit Sector* (Warsaw: Information Science Reference, 2015), 70.

[304] Social Media Group, "Going Social," 14; Campbell, "Steps to a Successful Nonprofit Social Media Strategy".

supporters are.[305] Hootsuite, Tweetdeck, and Twitalyzer are also good examples of tools you can use to keep track of keywords. In particular, Heather Mansfield, a well-known nonprofit social media communications advisor, recommends you follow larger nonprofits with similar missions since they have the resources to experiment online.[306]

Thirdly, referencing what other people have done is not just about sharing their content, but also building on the slang and conventional joke formats of hashtags, GIFS, memes, vines, and other content produced by others. For example, the anti-smoking nonprofit the Truth Initiative has been very effective at using hashtags, YouTube personalities, and vernacular in their campaign "#BigTobaccoBe-Like".[307] Do this badly and not only will you seem out of touch, but the social media platform algorithm may punish you, as we will soon discuss.[308]

Finally, advisors remind you that part of participating on the internet is giving up some control of your content.[309] Dialogue is not only possible but expected by your audience.[310] Users can share, comment, and alter content in unexpected ways. If enough people share your content, then it goes "viral". To get a video to go viral, advisors say that you should think about what it will say about the person sharing the video.[311] For example, will it help them look edgy or caring?

Social Media is Fast

The internet has also made it possible to distribute content at unprecedented speeds. This has made it so that even traditional media, such as newspapers, have to constantly update stories.[312] Twitter in particular is highlighted as a platform for "in the moment" sharing

[305] Campbell, "Steps to a Successful Nonprofit Social Media Strategy".
[306] Heather Mansfield, "Nonprofit Tech for Good".
[307] Alexandra, "5 Examples Of Nonprofit Social Media Strategies".
[308] Kanter, "Can Memes for Good Work for your Nonprofit's Content Strategy?"
[309] Williams, *Marketing & Communications*.
[310] Kinzey *Promoting nonprofit organizations*, 8.
[311] Alexandra, "5 Examples Of Nonprofit Social Media Strategies".
[312] Kinzey *Promoting nonprofit organizations*.

of information and views.[313] This speed is reflected in some advisors suggesting that you tweet at least twice a day, whereas you may only need to update your blog twice a month.[314] In any case, advisors tell you that, to keep people engaged, you need to update your channels regularly.[315] One way you can keep up is by reusing content you have already created for offline purposes.[316]

Relatedly, some advisors emphasize that the average attention span of your audience has become very short.[317] However, scholars have also found that long-format posts (1200-1500 words) are more likely to generate engagement.[318] This is in line with the advisors who advocate for a "content marketing" approach in which you draw attention by creating useful content.[319] Precisely because readers are so time-crunched, posting less frequently but with higher quality content is more likely to attract engagement.[320]

One way to cope with this speed is to invite guest bloggers to produce content for you.[321] Similarly, sharing other people's content is a great a way to distribute lots of content if you do not have much staff.[322]

Social Media is Controlled by Algorithms

Finally, many social media platforms organize the distribution of content according to centrally determined algorithms, which may seem like a new feature. What content succeeds on a social media platform is largely a result of its ability to appeal to the platform's "algorithms".[323] Algorithms are a way of sorting out what content

---

[313] Kinzey *Promoting nonprofit organizations*, 161.

[314] Social Media Group, "Going Social," 15.

[315] MissionBox Staff, "Drafting a Nonprofit Communications Strategy".

[316] Kinzey, *Promoting nonprofit organizations*, 157.

[317] Brinckhoff, *Mission-Based Marketing*, 71.

[318] Julia Carboni and Sarah Maxwell, "Effective Social Media Engagement for Non-profits: What matters?" *Journal of Public and Nonprofit Affairs*, 1 No 18 (2015).

[319] Azelrad, "The 9 Signs of a Successful Social Media Strategy for Nonprofits".

[320] Kinzey, *Promoting nonprofit organizations*, 156.

[321] Kinzey, *Promoting nonprofit organizations*, 154.

[322] David Chapman, "Social Media as a Tool for Nonprofit Advocacy and Civic Engagement," 73.

[323] Campbell, "Steps to a Successful Nonprofit Social Media Strategy".

will appear in a user's feed based on relevancy rather than publication time.[324] Different platforms emphasize different things. For example, Twitter emphasizes network diversity whereas Facebook tends to create bubbles.[325] As a result of the diversity of the algorithms, picking the right platform can be a crucial factor in your success.[326]

Scholars and policy makers have been criticizing the huge and non-transparent influence of these algorithms for a number of years now.[327] Some advisors do caution about the for-profit nature of these platforms.[328] But advisors mainly tell you what you need to do in order to appeal to these algorithms, so your content has a wider reach. Recommendations include:[329]

- Post more video
- Pay for advertisements
- Tailor your posts to each platform
- Link to authoritative sources from outside of Facebook (to avoid fake news)
- Imitate content that has received lots of engagement (comments, likes, shares, etc.)
- Brand your content with hashtags so it is more easily searchable.

Social media companies do change their algorithms. When they do, you will want to respond by understanding the substance of the change and altering your content to appeal to the new standards.

---

[324] Brent Barnhart, "Everything you need to know about social media algorithms," *SproutSocial* (August 13, 2019).

[325] Comunello, Mulargia, Parisi, "The 'Proper' Way to Spread Ideas through Social Media," 517.

[326] Comunello, Mulargia, Parisi, 517.

[327] Cecilia Jaques, Mine Islar, Gavin Lord, "Post-Truth: Hegemony on Social Media and Implications for Sustainability" *Communication and Sustainability*, 11 (2019): 2.

[328] Mansfield, Nonprofit Tech for Good, 69.

[329] Campbell "Steps to a Successful Nonprofit Social Media Strategy,"; Classy, "The Big Social Media Guide for Nonprofits"; Anderson, "How Nonprofits Can Use Measurement To Adapt to the Facebook Algorithm"; Dopson, "Social Media for Nonprofits".

THE PROBLEM: SOCIAL MEDIA IS NOT DIFFERENT

In past chapters I highlighted the limitations of conventional advice. In this chapter, I will contradict conventional advice less and instead show you how *The 100-Year PR Plan* fits into all the above advice. Firstly, I will explain that innovating ideologists have always recommended a visual approach to rhetoric. I will then provide an example of how we can apply Skinner's methods to images and videos online. Secondly, I will look at how the interactivity of social media relates to what I have already said about your relationship to broader movements. Thirdly, I will explain how speed affects what makes "useful" ideological change, and how despite the pressure of time, slow and valuable long-format content is still the gold standard. Finally, I will focus on the effect of having to appeal to a platform's algorithm. I will point out special opportunities in online educational platforms, and, if all else fails, creating your own online institutions.

Rhetoric Has Always Been Multimedia

Quentin Skinner states explicitly that his analysis of rhetoric applies beyond words.[330] Below, I explain what that means for how you approach photo and video content online.

Rhetoric Has Always Been Visual

Long before the internet, or even the television, rhetoricians realized that effective rhetoric is visual. Skinner cites the Roman rhetorician Quintilian who taught:

> *"You must find the means, as he likes to put it, to convert your auditors into spectators, presenting them with an image or picture 'that will lead them to feel they were present at the scene.' The effect of such verbal painting is that 'our passions are aroused just as much as if we were actually witnessing the events themselves'.*[331]

Rhetoricians did not just care about metaphors and similes but literal images as well. For example, Thomas Hobbes, a highly influential political thinker, cared a great deal about the covers of his books.[332] And

---

[330] Skinner, *Visions of Politics*, 134.
[331] Skinner, *From Humanism to Hobbes*, 6.
[332] Skinner, *From Humanism to Hobbes*, 222-315.

papers are still written about what messages those covers convey.[333]

In a similar way that words have a sense, reference, and judgment, so can images and symbols. Consequently, I would argue, it is possible to apply Skinner's analytic framework to images as well.[334]

Think about the logos of nonprofits. Whereas the image of a cross may have at one time expressed an unquestionably religious message, the symbol of the Red Cross today arguably is associated much more with a kind of religiously neutral humanitarianism. The secularization of the image of the cross may be like the secularization of the word religious (e.g., I watch football religiously).

Think about the images you use. What is their sense, reference, and judgment value? Are you using images that reinforce the prevalent understanding or are you innovating? Consider for example the campaign "Give a Shit" by WaterAid to raise awareness about global sanitation issues. The app shown below plays on changing attitudes towards feces embodied in "cute" emojis. This is very clever because it allows them to tap into a cultural change that allows them to present their issue as interesting and engaging in new ways. Furthermore, this is a great example of taking a seemingly apolitical change in language and putting it to political uses.

Source: visme.co[335]

---

[333] Thomas Poole, "Leviathan in Lockdown," *London Review of Books* (May 2020).

[334] Although Skinner suggests at a theoretical level that his framework applies to images, I am not aware of him actually applying his method directly to an image.

[335] Samantha Lile. "17 Creative Visual Marketing Campaigns by Nonprofits" (2017) https://visme.co/blog/nonprofit-marketing/.

Rhetoric Has Always Included Action

The same way that a person can change the sense, reference, and judgment of a word by speaking or an image by sharing, they can change the sense, reference, and judgment of an act by acting.[336]

Consider, for example, the Nazi salute (even without the statement "Heil Hitler"). The sense is clearly to pledge allegiance to Nazi ideology. Originally, it applied in a limited range of cases (e.g., as a greeting in Nazi Germany, in the military or at rallies, etc.). The judgment implied in it was clearly to endorse Nazi ideology. After the end of the Holocaust and especially after the salute was made illegal in Germany, it obviously took on very negative connotations, but therefore also took on connotations of counter-culture. Now, when it is used in GIFS (repetitive short videos) "ironically" or otherwise, this is a clear example of tactic 5 from Chapter 6's exercise "watering down a term" (or action) through repetition.[337] By using an action others use with disapproval positively (e.g., for humour) or neutrally (e.g., mindless repetition) you may force the audience to re-evaluate it (i.e., "that's pretty funny, what's the big deal?"). It then becomes easier to get them to re-evaluate the broader system of language or symbols that the act is taken from. Memes are a particularly effective medium for this tactic because memes are essentially about repetition.

This transformation is not only an example of watering down the term. Because of the counter-cultural connotations the gesture picked up since the Holocaust, it has become associated with "edgelord" internet subculture.[338] An edge lord is someone who discusses offensive or taboo topics to appear edgy. Unsurprisingly, therefore the salute as a gesture may be particularly "useful" to teenage boys as a way to assert independence and buttress their egos. Much has been written about how what begins as a joke becomes internalized.[339] Neo-Nazis have been able to capitalize on being able to serve this constituency in this way and thereby recruit them.

---

[336] Skinner, *Visions of Politics*, 134.

[337] Nazi Salute GIFS, Tenor https://tenor.com/search/nazi-salute-GIFS.

[338] Edgelord, Dictionary.com https://www.dictionary.com/e/slang/edgelord/.

[339] Molly Wood, More extremists are getting radicalized online. Whose responsibility is that? *Marketplace*, March 19, 2019.

The salute is just one example. My overall point is that we can apply Skinner's analysis of rhetoric to actions as well. This opens the door to being able to analyze a host of different web content, from GIFS and memes to videos. If we can usefully apply this approach to the alt-right GIFS, why not the Ice Bucket Challenge?

Rhetoric Has Always Interacted with What Was Already There

Above, I discussed how advisors tell you to be participatory, reference others, and jump on trends. In this subsection I will discuss how, following Skinner's theories, you may do this in a transformative way rather than simply a reactive way. Firstly, I will discuss how new technologies (particularly video games and online events) allow you to build ideological transformation into the very rules of participation. Secondly, I will discuss how innovating ideologists have always referenced others and what this means for the untapped potential of Wikipedia. Thirdly, I will discuss how to spot trends that offer potential for ideological transformation. Lastly, I will discuss the importance of building relationships between others, not just with you.

Encourage Participation: Persuading Through Games

Advisors recommend that you make content interactive. As I discussed above, interactivity ranges from simply asking a question, to offering a poll with defined choices, to organizing an event, to creating an online game. There is an idea in the study of video games called "procedural rhetoric". The idea is basically that you communicate not only in what you say or show people in the game, but that the rules of the game quietly get people to think the world works a certain way.[340]

Think back to Chapter 2, when we talked about how ideologies are not just keywords but the structures that connect the meaning of all these words together. The rules of a game (or an event you organize) tacitly build connections in the same way. There are some examples of nonprofits creating video games. For example, PETA created its

---

[340] Ian Bogost, "The Rhetoric of Video Games." *The Ecology of Games: Connecting Youth, Games, and Learning.* Ed. by Katie Salen. The John D. and Catherine T. MacArthur Foundation Series on Digital Media and Learning. (Cambridge, MA: The MIT Press, 2008): 117–40.

own Pokémon game.[341] The text and images both clearly express their message, but the rules of the game do too. In regular Pokémon, the Pokémon only fight each other. In this game, the Pokémon fight humans. This clearly expresses an innovation in terms of who the enemies are. Nonprofits have just begun to scratch the surface of what video games have to offer.

You don't need to create a video game to tap into the power of procedural rhetoric. If you run a group, think about what community rules (expressed or unexpressed) are. If you organize an event, think about what the rules of engagement will be. For example, will one person speak, and others respond (e.g., an Ask Me Anything event on Reddit or streaming), or will everyone have a chance to speak (e.g., a Twitter storm or Google Hangout). What rules you set will send very different messages.

Referencing Others and the Untapped Potential of Wikipedia

That advisors recommend you reference the work of others should not surprise us. As discussed at length in past chapters, it is crucial that you build on the existing work of others to advance long-term transformation. In general, I therefore agree with what advisors have said, but before I discuss this topic in general, I want to highlight one platform that was completely ignored in the sources I reviewed.

Wikipedia holds enormous untapped potential for nonprofits as a tool of long-term societal transformation. To be clear, Wikipedia rules restrict advocacy.[342] I am not suggesting that nonprofits overtly or covertly violate these rules thus undermining this invaluable resource. So how can Wikipedia be useful? In Chapter 6, I discussed the tactic of appealing to an obscure or forgotten historical figure, event, or text to serve as an ideological rallying cry. If nonprofits want to use this tactic, it is crucial that the public become acquainted with that figure, event or text. One effective way to do this is to make sure that Wikipedia has a detailed and balanced article on that topic to help the public learn more.

This tactic has historical precedent. When the printing press

---

[341] PETA Pokémon Black and Blue https://games.peta.org/pokemon-black-and-white-parody/.

[342] Wikipedia, "advocacy" https://en.wikipedia.org/wiki/Wikipedia:Advocacy.

was first invented, Skinner writes, humanists were some of the first to realize its potential.[343] It was humanists who organized the first installation of the printing press in the basement of the Sorbonne (a renowned university in France). What potential did they see? Was it simply a tool to spread their own writing farther? Not primarily. They did not simply print their "propaganda". Rather, they made cheap and easily accessible translations of old works like those of Cicero. This increased the public's interest in the classics and therefore humanism.

Beyond Wikipedia, you should always look for opportunities to amplify the voices you identified in Chapter 7 as being crucial allies. And like in Chapter 3, you should not always be concerned if the platform is anonymous or collaborative.

The fluidity of social media means you should not feel restricted only to those who are posting on your topic of interest. You can easily build bridges to the other movements we talked about that have an interest in innovating the way you are innovating. A lot of advisors talk as if you should mainly produce your own content and supplement it with the content of others. But I think Skinner's discussion of the printing press shows that you should start with retweeting, reblogging, and sharing, and focus on adding comments that put it in the light your innovation needs. You should post original content as a way to supplement this, not the other way around.

Elsewhere, I have called this ability to speak through others a modern vow of silence.[344] The paradox of our age is that our power to create original content has never been greater, and yet it has never been easier to speak exclusively in terms of what others have already said. Many advisors talk about the noise that your audience faces, yet few recommend that you refrain from adding to it. Amplifying what your audience is already hearing is one of the most basic ways to turn the noise into harmony.

As I wrote earlier, one should not be more innovative than one has to be, and this means not producing new content for its own sake when the same goal can be accomplished by strengthening existing content. Whether this will bring greater attention and support to your

[343] Skinner, *The Foundations of Modern Political Thought*, 196.
[344] Miller, "The Temptations of Modern Silence." *Half a Maven* (July 9, 2017).

nonprofit in particular is an empirical question I cannot answer. It all goes back to defining your ultimate goal for social media. If it is to advance the organization, the above *may* not be a good strategy. But if it is to advance long-term ideological innovation, there are some good reasons to think building as much as possible on the work of others will strengthen your cause.

Effective Rhetoric Understands the Vernacular

In Chapter 2, I emphasized that every revolutionary needs to march into battle backwards. This means that while you are innovating, you are also going to be dependent on the existing moral language of the people you are appealing to. This is almost comically true when it comes to social media. Every subgroup of every platform seems to have its own language. If you do not understand the language of the platform, such as slang or running jokes, but you try to use it, you will come off as insincere and out of touch. In many quarters, you may also be mercilessly ridiculed. We already saw above WaterAid use emojis to good effect.

Another good example of working with existing online tropes (coincidentally also from the international development sector focused on water) is what the nonprofit WATERisLIFE did with the #firstworldproblems trend. The hashtag is a joke in which people complain about minor problems that could only happen to privileged people. WATERisLIFE shared a video of people in their "third world" homes reading these tweets. It was wildly successful.[345] I would argue that this is because it exploited an inner tension already implicit in the moral language of the hashtag. The joke itself depends on the guilt of the subject for being in a privileged position.

The lesson we can take from this is that online trends are a great place to look for expressions of existing tensions in moral vocabulary that we identified is Chapter 6 as being ripe for change. The WATERisLIFE campaign arguably did not innovate the meaning of any of the terms, but it is still a good example of spotting potential to exploit existing tensions.

---

[345] Alexandra, "5 Examples Of Nonprofit Social Media Strategies".

I hate it when my house is so big, I need two wireless routers.

Photo source: CNN.com[346]

A more nefarious example of innovative meme use was the alt-right's use of the evil Kermit meme during the last American election.[347] The meme involves Kermit the Frog staring at his evil doppelganger from one of the Muppets films. The joke is supposed to be that this image represents someone giving into an impulse they know they should reject, such as buying something they don't need. The alt-right used it to promote its political objectives. This was a very clever use of the meme because it aligns a typical view of racism (as an impulse to be suppressed) with consumerist behaviour. Much advertising encourages us to give into guilty pleasures, so people are used to giving in.[348] The alt-right was simply redirecting that encouragement towards racist behaviours with apparent success.

ME: I HATE ALARMIST, POPULIST, RACIST, XENOPHOBIC AND SEXIST VIEWS

OTHER ME: VOTE TRUMP

[346] Ed Payne and Chandler Friedman, "Viral ad campaign hits #FirstWorldProblems," *CNN*, October 23, 2012.

[347] Allie Volpe, "It's not all Pepes and trollfaces — memes can be a force for good," *The Verge*, August 27, 2018.

[348] Paul Hiebert, "Here's Why Ads That Celebrate Eating in Secret Work," *AdWeek*, December 2, 2019.

The message here is that you do not need to rack your brain coming up with the next big thing. Look at what is already out there with an eye towards the vulnerabilities and opportunities for change that you have already identified in prevailing moral vocabularies. If you can come up with a moderately clever way to exploit those tensions to further your end, if you do go viral, it will likely be more than just 5 seconds of fame.

Giving Up Control, Building Relationships

Finally, advisors warn you that interactivity online means you need to give up control of the content. This should sit well with our discussion in Chapter 3 and the need to de-centre your organization. Ideological innovation has only ever been possible by connecting people to one another.

For example, Skinner tells the story of how humanism gained a foothold in England. Duke Humphrey of Gloucester hired Pietro Del Monte as a literary advisor.[349] Pietro then introduced the Duke to many great works of humanist scholarship as well as humanist scholars. After decades of collecting these works, the Duke eventually dedicated hundreds of them to the University of Oxford, thus making them available to the public and spreading the ideas throughout England.

The point to observe is that Pietro was an agent of change not because he connected others to himself, but because he brought together others who would in turn have a big influence. As we saw above, advisors often talk about how nonprofits use social media as a tool to build relationships with supporters and other organizations. This is of course an important step in long-term transformation. However, it is important not to forget that social media also offers the potential to connect other people to each other. Rather than always having to initiate the conversation, Jennifer Ihm, a nonprofit communications scholar, has observed that nonprofits can create "stakeholder autonomous networks" where the community continues on its own momentum.[350]

---

[349] Skinner, *The Foundations of Modern Political Thought*, 195.

[350] J. Ihm, "Communicating without nonprofit organizations on nonprofits' social media: Stakeholders' autonomous networks and three types of organizational ties," *New Media & Society*, 21 No 11–12 (2019): 2648–2670.

Don't Be in Such a Rush

We saw above that advisors both encourage you to post often but also emphasize the value of high-quality less frequent content. In this subsection, I explain how you should see the value in both slow and fast content. At the end of Chapter 6's exercise, I identified two types of communications channels. The first is where you make the case explicitly for a linguistic innovation. Ideally, this is done through slow long-format content. The second is where you propagate an innovation simply through repetition. This is perfect for fast content.

Speed and the Professional Interests of Journalists

The time pressures of social media do not just apply to nonprofits but to journalists as well. This pressure on journalists has led to their increasing dependence on prepackaged content.[351] This has given nonprofits, as well as others, new abilities to leverage the traditional media to communicate their message. In some ways this is a new development.

But remember, in the last chapter we discussed how the crucial factor that will determine the success of one ideological innovation over another is its usefulness. Furthermore, I specifically pointed out how you can make your innovations useful to not only a school of thought but to a profession as well. Creating news content that fills the needs of journalists, in principle, is no different. You will want to write in a way that conforms to their style and is easily communicated in their format, but fundamentally the goal is simply to be useful to them.

Consider, for example, cancel culture. I have no doubt that there are many factors behind its success. I would argue that one of them is the simple narrative arc every story of cancel culture shares.

- Celebrity A said/does X.
- Group Y (including other celebrities) found X objectionable and began shaming Celebrity A.
- Group Z (including other celebrities) defends X.
- Celebrity A either apologizes or doubles down.

---

[351] Ongenaert, *Refugee Organizations,* 195–206.

Insert a few witty tweets from members of either group and I suspect you could put together a sufficiently polished and interesting 750-word article in under an hour. The characters are easily recognizable. There may be a clear resolution or the promise of a continued drama. The best part about it is that each individual instance of cancel culture is its own story, but by clearly demonstrating the tropes of cancel culture it reinforces the broader story.

The above is not meant to be flippant nor to detract from the important issues that may be at stake in any particular cancel culture story. Rather, I am pointing out that the media industry, like most other industries today, operates on a model of mass production. The greater volume of easily reproducible stories a particular term can generate (by labelling it in a way that makes it a known commodity), the more attractive it will be to the tired freelance workers whose livelihood depends on their speed at the assembly line of words.

Playing the Long-Game on Twitter

I mentioned above that Twitter is seen by some as especially requiring speed. "Twitter storms" explode so quickly online that I think nonprofits often share the "fear of missing out" (FOMO) that is said to motivate so many other social media users. Not wanting to be a Johnny-come-lately, you may always want to be an early adopter of budding hashtags.

If that sounds like your situation, then no doubt you are exhausted from trying to keep up. It's funny that advisors often talk about how your audience faces so much confusing noise, but rarely mention how you face the same noise too. How are you supposed to know what trends to follow? When are you supposed to jump in? And most importantly, how can you go viral?

Going viral is nothing new. One could easily argue that that's exactly what Skinner studies. The difference is that after a movement has spread, it needs to seep into the existing institutions and behaviours in order to have a long-term impact. How then can you engage in a way that will not only go viral but will also stick? If you followed the steps in the first half of this book, you would have greater focus in both going viral and sticking around.

Firstly, you will know who to follow because you will know precisely what words to keep track of, and who your potential allies and competitors are. Secondly, you will observe that going viral is easier when (a) there is a pre-existing network, and (b) the hashtag helps people in the network, as well as potential allies (such as press), do something. To illustrate this point, let us consider the case of the #MeToo movement through the lens of *The 100-Year PR Plan*.

If you are interested in gender-based violence (GBV), then you will no doubt follow many organizations and activists working on that issue. You would have therefore noticed sooner or later the #MeToo and #BeenRapedNeverReported. The core of the pre-existing "network" (although they may not all be formally connected on Twitter) was the massive number of women who have experienced sexual violence at the hands of men. You would also have noticed that women were saying the same things they have been saying for decades. In fact, the slogan itself had already been coined back in 2006, over a decade before the hashtag took off.[352] Consequently, it could fairly be said that this was building on decades of pre-existing ideas, attitudes, and organizing.

How, if at all, did Twitter make a difference to the women's movement that had already been doing this work for so long? I would argue two things. Firstly, the fact that in the catalyst case *both* the survivor (Ashley Judd) and the perpetrator (Harvey Weinstein) were celebrities made it more attractive for the press.[353] Secondly, Twitter itself acted as a high-powered aggregator of succinct and shocking personal stories that only continued to grow. Each tweet was easily accessible through the trending function of Twitter, reaching its own network through the personal account of the poster, and being amplified by others. Furthermore, the way in which it poured out over time, instead of, for example, being published in a single massive report, also allowed it to sustain interest and attention. In some senses, therefore it was an excellent medium for telling a story that was both overwhelmingly systemic and deeply personal without compromising

[352] Me Too Movement, (2020) https://metoomvmt.org/about/.
[353] Chicago Tribune, "#MeToo: A timeline of events, 2017-2020" *Chicago Tribune*, September 17, 2020; Abby Ohlheiser, "How #MeToo really was different according to data," *The Washington Post*, October 7, 2018.

either aspect (as many other mediums, such as official reports, often struggle to do).

Experts have said it is too soon to tell the long-term impact of the movement,[354] although there have already been promising signs.[355] But using the lessons of *The 100-Year PR Plan*, we see a number of reasons to expect it will have a long-term impact. Firstly, gender-based violence is a wrong which is clearly recognizable in the existing prevalent moral language. Secondly, the public accusation that the hashtag represents is capable of leveraging material consequences for individual men and organizations even if they do not believe in it. Thirdly, there are institutions in the world who have an interest in and are capable of carrying this work forward, if only because it affirms the importance of their work (most notably lawyers and HR professionals).[356] Fourthly, although survivors who report violence still face reprisals, pushback, disrespect, and much else, the collective umbrella seems to have provided many with encouragement and protection needed to allow them to do something that is vital to their healing, disclosing their experience.[357] This makes it a useful hashtag, and the phenomenon it created a useful moment for many women.

This whole discussion is just to show that what makes Twitter campaigns truly effective is built up over decades and must be carried forward over years. The speed of the moment is misleading. Incidentally, this insight may also answer the critics of "slacktivism". Solely online action may not in itself have the ability to accomplish its goals if it is not embedded in offline networks and institutions with the capacity to carry the ideological innovation forward into the world. I admit though, much of this is speculative and is mainly offered as food for thought.

---

[354] Courtney Akerley, "What Will Be the Long-Term Impact of the #MeToo Movement?" University of Connecticut November 5, 2018.

[355] Anna North, "7 positive changes that have come from the #MeToo movement." *Vox*, October 4, 2019.

[356] Camille Hebert, "Is MeToo Only a Social Movement Or a Legal Movement Too," Employee Rights and Employment Policy Journal, 22 No. 2 (2018): 321.

[357] Roee Levy, Martin Mattsson, "The Effects of Social Movements: Evidence from #MeToo," (Working Paper, Yale University, March 30, 2020).

Long-Format Content FTW!

I discussed above how scholars have found long-format content leads to more user engagement. The paradox of the past couple years is that at the same time that 3-second GIFS have been exploding, so have long-format podcasts.[358] On average 45 minutes, "a remarkable attentiveness measure according to Edison Research, is that 85% of people who listen to podcasts, listen to the end."[359]

I think the lesson here is that you do not need to condescend to your audience. Short-form content has much to contribute. As I wrote earlier, citing Dewey, the legacy of some of the most influential books in the West have been a few pithy phrases. But it's important the whole book was written first to give depth to those phrases. Take a page out of the civic humanist playbook that Skinner studied; while others wrote guides to princes and civil servants, they wrote books to the public.[360]

Don't be afraid to write substantial things geared towards the public. People have always been hungry to learn. In addition to podcasts, the success of online courses and e-books shows that people want to learn outside of formal institutions.[361] Nonprofits and social movements have tapped into this in the past.

For example, in the 70s, the free university movement gave rise to hundreds of nonprofits across the United States that delivered adult education classes.[362] The organizations varied in many ways but kept a philosophy that teaching and learning should be free and done for its own sake. These organizations posed an intrinsic challenge to the "educational-industrial complex" that they saw in the mainstream universities. Furthermore, because anyone was free to teach anything, these were ideal sites for disseminating all kinds of ideas. These

---

[358] Michelle Greenwald, "What's Really Driving the Limitless Growth Of Podcasts," *Forbes*, October 4, 2018.

[359] Greenwald, "What's Really Driving the Limitless Growth Of Podcasts".

[360] Skinner, *The Foundations of Modern Political Thought*, 215.

[361] Lewis Keegan, "79+ Staggering Online Learning Statistics! (All You Need To Know!)," *Skillscouter*, May 7, 2020; Statista, eBooks-Worldwide (2020) https://www.statista.com/outlook/213/100/ebooks/worldwide.

[362] Bill Draves, "The Free University: A Model for Lifelong Learning," (Chicago: Association Press, Follett Publishing Company, 1980).

schools therefore acted as nodes in broader networks connecting many different movements.

But for the fact that they are for the most part corporately owned and controlled, social media networks, such as YouTube, have managed to serve a similar purpose. And you can tap into this impulse by developing genuine educational content online that makes the case for your innovation. This takes time and the right people, though, and we will discuss this further below as we discuss the issue of corporate control of the platform.

Central Control of Platform is Not New

For decades, scholars have observed how nonprofits have had to conform to dominant media logic in order to get their stories in the mainstream press.[363] The fact that this media logic is now rigidly programmed in the form of an algorithm may make it more inflexible, but it does not fundamentally change what nonprofits have to do. Nonprofits have always faced three options when it comes to interacting with the values of dominant institutions. You can either conform to those values, contend for control of those institutions, or try to form your own. Social media is no different. Below, I will consider the latter two options with a special focus on online education.

The Special Importance of Educational Institutions Online (Especially Now)

Skinner's story about the spread of humanism or Lutheranism, for example, emphasizes the important roles universities (and law schools in particular) played as long-term disseminators of each school of thought.[364] In some cases, the innovators came to existing universities and seized control from existing dominant ways of thinking. In other cases, new universities opened up and served as disseminators from the beginning.

In Chapter 4, I talked about how your organization does not need to survive in the long term for you to have a big long-term impact. But that does not mean the broader movement can succeed without some long-lived institutions. For example, Skinner points to Fausto

---

[363] Ongenaert, "Refugee Organizations".

[364] Skinner, *The Foundations of Modern Political Thought*, 50-54.

Andrelini's 30 years of scholarship at the University of Paris, which did more than anyone else to allow humanism to triumph over scholasticism at that institution.[365] The University of Paris would go on to be a beacon of humanist learning, training generations of leaders.

Universities and colleges, of course, remain important, especially since far more people attend them today than ever before. Especially in the post-COVID context, education will increasingly take place online. In the near future, therefore, schools will increasingly be looking for online content. Academic staff are already operating on a precarious contract model. I suspect the result will be that these institutions will be particularly open to the influence of external parties engaged in ideological contest through creating online educational material.

Above, I mentioned how advisors encourage "content marketing strategies" (i.e., producing useful content). I would like to take that a step further and say that textbooks, guides, and online courses created for traditional institutions (such as schools and workplaces) offer a special potential for long-term ideological transformation. As I discussed above, advisors to nonprofits have not yet begun to scratch the surface of Wikipedia's full potential. I would add that this also applies to websites for sharing open source educational materials (such as textbooks).

There has never been a better time for nonprofits to get involved in this kind of long-term transformative work. As an increasing number of individuals with PhDs look for work outside universities, the nonprofit sector has the opportunity to absorb this talent.[366] Assuming you have the funds, you may have the potential to recruit PhDs who are experts in a subject or perspective of importance to your work. You can provide them with an institutional context to continue their work, and they can create educational products with sufficient rigour to be useful to educational institutions. These products will benefit from the stability and credibility of pre-existing offline institutions that are now seeking to add more online content.

What sort of content do I mean? Quentin Skinner gives the

---

[365] Skinner, *The Foundations of Modern Political Thought*, 194.

[366] Janay Cody, Ph.D., "Why PhDs Shouldn't Overlook A Career With A Nonprofit Organization." *Cheeky Scientist* (2020); "Guest Blogs by Sector: Non-Profit, *PhDs at Work*".

example of rhetoricians who wrote textbooks for those training to be civil servants.[367] They would give examples of the proper way to write a letter or a speech. In the appendix of these textbooks, they would include samples of letters and speeches that would essentially convey their opinion on various issues of the day. Eventually, after decades, these teachers explicitly presented themselves as political advisors. This is a bit too on the nose but publishing relevant textbooks in your area does make it easier for others to teach it and for students to take an interest in it.

These strategies have not been forgotten. Jane Mayer, in her book "Dark Money" describes how Richard Mellon Scaife, the Koch Brothers, and others advanced ideological objectives by funding "law and economics fellowships" at law schools, creating an economics curriculum for under-funded high schools, and more.[368] These tactics have been highly successful, and law and economics is now one of the dominant schools of thought in the study of law. Furthermore, the university presence allows them to recruit university students into their network of advocacy groups under the guise of neutral education.

I feel compelled to make a distinction at this point. There is a difference between a carefully planned ideological innovation winning over the allegiance of academic institutions through its usefulness and intellectual rigour, and essentially buying your way into schools. I do not recommend the latter approach, because it is ethically dubious and ultimately undermines the credibility of the educational institutions it depends on.

Nevertheless, I want to highlight that this active ideological contest for academic institutions is by no means a recent development, and it is still a contest waged to great effect. And we may be entering a moment of greater potential in this area. Nonprofits who genuinely care about the issues they work on would do well to partner with sincerely motivated academically trained individuals to correct the limitations of what is currently taught in schools.

---

[367] Skinner, *The Foundations of Modern Political Thought,* 213; Skinner, 31.

[368] Benjamin Miller, "Striking the Right Regulatory Balance May be Key to Helping Canada Avoid the Creep of 'Dark Money' that has Infiltrated Politics and Philanthropy South of the Border" *The Philanthropist*, March 2, 2020.

Creating Your Own Institutions

If you can't join 'em beat 'em. This is certainly true in social media, where it is much easier to build a website than it is to purchase a new headquarters. In the online context, it may be too early to tell if any institutions offer a sufficiently stable long-term institutional structure to steward ideological innovations on their own. Nevertheless, if any online infrastructure is to play this role, it will likely be the platforms themselves, and in some cases the communities on the platforms (e.g., Facebook groups or subReddits). You may, therefore, want to create your own if you truly cannot find a place in the existing networks.

For example, members of the far-right who were either banned or discontented with the rules of more mainstream platforms created Gab.[369] It has since become a haven for the alt-right and has grown in both membership and intensity.[370] Gab is only the latest of a long line of social media platforms that have catered to hate speech, each of which have been shut down for various legal reasons or failing due to inner turmoil.[371] These institutions are largely defined by their moderating policies.

On the other side of the political spectrum, we find Tumblr. It is a highly visual network and has served as the institutional home of a distinct form of contemporary feminism. According to some, it is the first wave of feminism to be based in visual philosophy,[372] or, if you prefer, visual rhetoric.

Both examples demonstrate that it is possible for movements to both actively create their own or occupy existing online infrastructure. I have not found any examples of nonprofits actively creating these spaces, but as the central control of platforms becomes increasingly

---

[369] Reid McIlroy-Young, Ashton Anderson, "From 'Welcome New Gabbers' to the Pittsburgh Synagogue Shooting: The Evolution of Gab," *Proceedings of the International AAAI Conference on Web and Social Media*, 13 No 1 (December 24, 2019): 651-654.

[370] McIlroy-Young, Anderson, "From 'Welcome New Gabbers'".

[371] David Gilbert, "Here's How Big Far Right Social Network Gab Has Actually Gotten," *Vice*, August 16, 2019; Joanne McNeil, "From Anon to Alt-Right: The Dangerous Tricksters of 4chan On the Evolution of Online Toxicity," *Literary Hub*, March 2, 2020.

[372] Text Ione Gamble, "In Defence of Tumblr Feminism," *Dazed*, April 8, 2016.

problematic for society, you may find it necessary at some point in the future to create alternatives.

THE SOLUTION: OBSERVING COMMUNITIES AND TRENDS

In Part 2, I drew on a lot of the lessons we learned in past chapters. Below, I organize these lessons so you can implement them more easily.

Step 1: What to Listen For

As the advisors tell you, social media engagement begins by listening. Look back of the web of words you identified in Chapter 2. Use Google Alerts and other tracking programs to follow the keywords and phrases you identified. You want to be tracking examples of memes, hashtags, and expressions that express the inner tension in existing moral vocabularies that you identified in Chapter 4.

Step 2: Who to Listen To

You want to be actively participating in existing networks by commenting and referencing the content of others. You need to really absorb not just what others say but how they say it. Based on our discussion in Chapters 6 and 7, there are four basic types of people and organizations you want to follow:

- Decision-makers you are trying to influence
- Those who influence them (e.g., who they follow but also the "silent opposition" we talked about)
- Potential allies both working on your issue and other issues
- Ideological competitors working on your issue.

Once you have "creeped" long enough by listening to these, then you can start thinking about posting.

Step 3: Repost Before Posting

In Chapter 7, we discussed how to identify other organizations who are using words in ways that advance the ideological innovation you have in mind. Reposting their content is therefore a good idea. You can comment to show your support or in ways that reinforce the innovation. Remember to think outside the box and, where appropriate, share the messages of those working on other issues but who are seeking similar ideological change to you.

You do not need to limit yourself to sharing content from people who are active on social media. In Chapter 6, we discussed the tactic of drawing on the names and works of historical figures. You can share links to articles about them, link to their original content, recommend new books about them, or other similar posts.

Overall, you want to start with other people's content and save your original posts for when it truly adds value or fills a gap in the existing conversation.

Step 4: Communicating Visually

Remember Chapter 4's exercise where I asked you to communicate the justification for your end goal in conventional language? Now translate that justification into an image. It could be a graph, infographic, photo, video, or meme. Try out different mediums and see if you can better communicate in any particular form, which might dictate what platforms you focus on.

Look through libraries of existing memes, GIFS, and emojis to see if any of them capture ideas that are important to your message (e.g., the way WaterAid used the poop emoji).

For example, I took a quick glance at memes.com and the following caught my eye.

By swapping out one of these photos, this meme can be repurposed by including photos of figures who are identified with your innovation.

People with zero haters

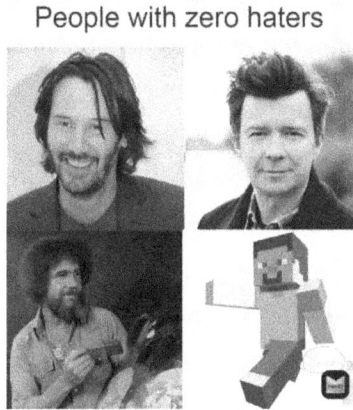

This meme has great potential because it basically asserts that things have changed through a play on words.

1. Put some folk wisdom at the top that represents an idea you are trying to dispel

2. Insert a comical photo which shows it disproven (e.g., through a visual pun)

3. Insert the photo seen in this meme "The future is now, old man."

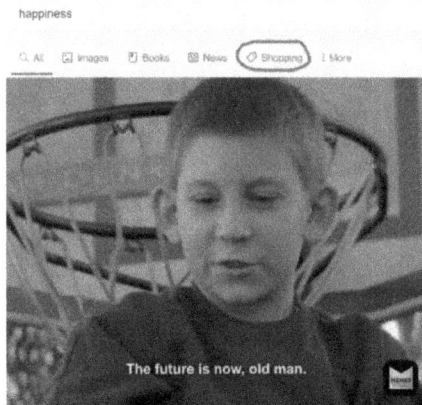

This meme is a great structure where you want to comically distinguish between two groups. Obviously, it is not appropriate where you want to dispel distinctions. You could swap out the images of "girls" and "boys" for anything else and have them talk to each other similarly. For example, two for-profits and non-profits, gas and electric vehicles, etc.

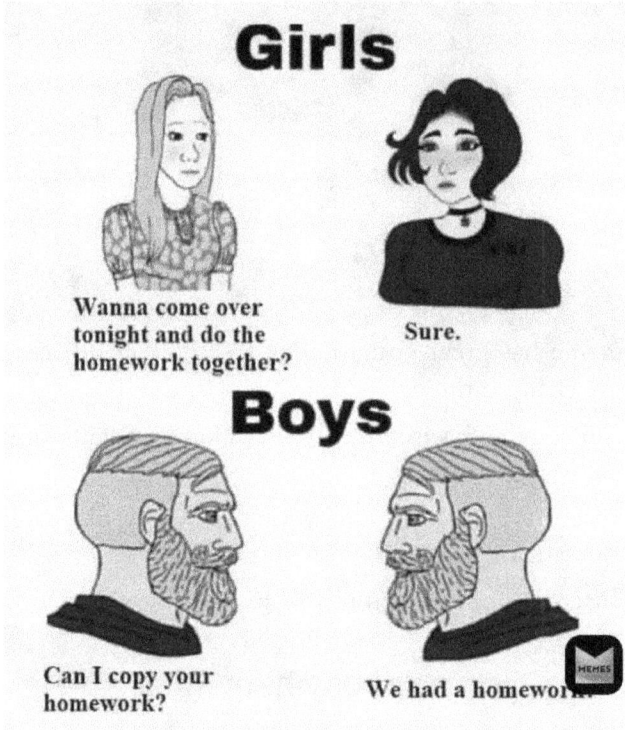

Girls

Wanna come over tonight and do the homework together?

Sure.

Boys

Can I copy your homework?

We had a homework?

This meme is much simpler to use than those above. Essentially, the joke is a minor annoyance that you comically elevate to "worse than the devil". It affirms the common feeling that something is bad while relieving the guilt for the complaint through a self-conscious acknowledgment of over-reaction (thereby denying the ability of the critic to make the accusation). It is therefore well suited to delegitimize actions that are admittedly minor but are symbolic of a broader system.

Youtube: Puts two unskippable ads before a video

Satan:

Even I'm not into that sl▨▨▨

This is also a very simple meme to use. Simply insert a pie chart representing a comically exaggerated version of a claim that supports the opposing view.

Step 5: Content Marketing is Your Friend

When you do post original content, don't be afraid to make it less frequent, longer, and higher quality. I think our discussion at the end of Chapter 7 means you should think like a content marketer. Produce expressions, tools, guides, courses, and more that are useful to ideological allies and foes alike. Where it is ethical to do so, target your content to traditional learning institutions.

Think about ways you can use your keywords in hashtags to label stories you want noticed in way that will make it easier for journalists to cover them. In particular, think about how you can break down the occurrence you are interested in into easily reproducible elements.

Step 6: Anonymous Transformation

Our discussion in Chapter 4 should have made clear that you should not be afraid to communicate anonymously. Learn how to contribute to Wikipedia, especially if you will be drawing on individuals, events, or concepts that do not already have a detailed and balanced page on the site.

Step 7: Where All Else Fails, Build Your Own House

If the algorithms of existing platforms simply make it impossible for your message to get traction, or if your mission makes it problematic to increase the power of a for-profit platform, then consider building an alternative platform or contributing to a more niche community. This is a last resort, but it is worth mentioning because existing institutions will always have limits.

Chapter 9

You Need Crisis

"Never waste a good crisis."

—Winston Churchill

Crisis management advice is usually about two types of crisis: controversies and emergencies.[373] In this chapter I will be talking about crises of legitimacy. We will look at how relevant typical crisis planning is for crises of legitimacy. The exercise in this chapter will be creating your very own legitimacy crisis plan.

In this chapter you will learn:

- How to make a conventional crisis plan
- Why crises are sometimes necessary for change
- How to bring about, sustain, and make the most of productive crises of legitimacy.

CONVENTIONAL WISDOM: CRISIS AS A REPUTATIONAL PROBLEM

In this section, I will look at four things. Firstly, I will look at what

---

[373] Patterson and Radtke, *Strategic Communications*, 16.

kind of crisis communications advice is designed for. We will see that whether it is a controversy or an emergency, a crisis is normally defined by a significant level of public interest and disruption in your nonprofit's work. We will then look at what advisors say you can do before, during, and after a crisis to prevent and mitigate it, in order to ultimately get back to normal (which is often the implied goal).

Before the crisis, you should think about the different possible crises and prioritize according to likelihood, impact, and controllability. You will then want to make a plan that clearly assigns roles and determines as best you can what you would say in such a situation.

During the crisis, advisors consistently tell you to put out a tentative message, then constantly gather information to quickly replace it with a consistent and more tailored response. You must be careful to combat any misinformation. Finally, after the crisis, it is important to take stock, measure the impact of the crisis, and keep pressure on action even though it is "over".

Defining Crisis: Controversy or Emergency

When advisors talk about crisis, they often mean a crisis *for* the organization.[374] Sally Patterson and Janel Radtke call these two types of crises: controversies and emergencies.[375]

A controversy is a crisis that threatens your nonprofit's reputation such as fraud or sexual harassment allegations. Emergencies include "predictable events that cause havoc for an organization or the people it serves and that may harm its ability to perform its mission."[376] Even when it is a general crisis, such as an economic downturn, this can be viewed through the lens of what impact it will have on the organization.[377] This of course is understandable. COVID-19 is a crisis for the world, but it is also a crisis for nonprofits as it seriously affects their finances, operations, staff, and volunteers.

Ruth Ellen Kinzey, author of *Promoting Nonprofit Organizations: A Reputation Management Approach*, observes that even though crises

---

[374] Tatiana Morand. "How to Create a Crisis Communications Plan for Your Nonprofit." *Wild Apricot*, March 20, 2020.

[375] Patterson and Radtke, *Strategic Communications*.

[376] Patterson and Radtke, *Strategic Communications*.

[377] Kinzey, *Promoting nonprofit organizations*, 25-26.

are unpredictable, they are usually certain to happen sometime.[378] She further observes that crises are heavily steeped in public perception, not necessarily logic. For example, an event that would have been a nonissue in a past generation, because of social media now may be elevated to a crisis.[379] Public perceptions may be particularly sensitive if your nonprofit has done something troubling that recently gave rise to a much bigger scandal elsewhere (e.g., sexual harassment during the height of the #MeToo movement).[380]

How will you know when something has shifted from a mere issue to a serious crisis? Look at these factors:

- Is it disrupting your day to day work?
- Are your ordinary processes unable to adequately respond to the issue?
- Is there an increasing amount of media/public attention you would not normally have?
- If left alone, would this have a long-term negative impact on the organization?[381]

Each of these is an indicator that an issue has escalated to a crisis. Ruth Ellen Kinzey also notes that crises operate on a condensed timeline and make uncertainty the new norm for the organization. Ultimately though, each crisis is also an opportunity to prove the nonprofit's value (e.g., in weathering the storm).[382]

Pre-Crisis: Prevent and Mitigate by Planning

According to the conventional approach, the major step you should take to prepare for a crisis is to have a crisis communication plan. The purpose of this plan is to prevent and mitigate the crisis as much as possible by ensuring there is clear responsibility for communicating

---

[378] Kinzey, 88-89.

[379] Kinzey, 90.

[380] Kinzey, 90.

[381] Meg Shannon, "How to create a crisis communications plan for your nonprofit organization," *Nonprofit Mar Community*, December 3, 2015.

[382] Shannon, "How to create a crisis communications plan for your nonprofit organization".

and the message is determined in advance as much as possible.[383] You can accomplish these goals by figuring out how to present a bad situation in the best light possible.[384] Ultimately, you are trying to preserve your nonprofit's reputation as a leader.[385] Ideally, the crisis communications plan should be formulated by a cross-section of people with different skill sets who work or volunteer with your nonprofit.[386]

In order to prepare for crisis communications, advisors recommend you create a crisis communications plan.[387] According to Patterson and Radtke, creators of a popular 7-step strategic communications plan, the crisis communications plan should answer the following questions:[388]

1. Who is responsible for managing the crisis, and what are his or her duties?

2. Where should the command center be for responding to the crisis?

3. What resources will be needed?

4. Who should be part of the crisis control team, and what are their responsibilities?

5. What information is appropriate to give to the public?

6. Who will speak for the organization? (it is especially important that you appoint a spokesperson for the organization, as well as a back-up spokesperson if they are not available.[389])

Another approach to the crisis communications plan, following Ruth Ellen Kinzey, is to think of it as a kind of manual and include

---

[383] Kinzey, 91.

[384] Nonprofit Risk Management Center, "Communicating During a Crisis," (2020).

[385] Colorado Nonprofit Association, "Crisis Communication Plan Nonprofit Toolkit"(n.d.), 2.

[386] Shea Davis, "How to Handle Crisis Communication. Nonprofit Communications Report," 15 No 2 (January 12, 2017): 7; Tatiana Morand, "How to create a communications plan for your nonprofit".

[387] Kinzey, *Promoting nonprofit organizations*, 85.

[388] Patterson and Radtke, *Strategic Communications*.

[389] Kinzey, 3.

the following information:[390]

1. Brief introduction explaining how to use the manual
2. Crisis communication objectives and guiding principles
3. Issue and risk identification research
4. initial response procedures and checklists
5. Media/public relations materials (e.g., fact sheets, graphs, visuals, etc.)
6. Contact lists

In order to make this plan, it is crucial that you bring together a crisis communication planning committee to brainstorm what possible crises could happen and then decide who will be responsible for implementing the plan.[391] It can be helpful to do a strengths/weaknesses/opportunities/challenges (SWOC) analysis to identify which crises are the most likely to occur.[392] You will then want to rank them according to likelihood, severity and controllability.[393] The goal is not to be exhaustive, only to get the most obvious crises.[394] You will want to focus your prevention efforts on those most severe and most controllable crises.

When predicting possible problems, your team should also predict possible storylines that the media will be interested in.[395] Building rapport with journalists ahead of time will make it easier to communicate with them in a crisis.[396]

Media is key in a crisis, and therefore much of your crisis communications depends on how you communicate with the media.[397] You should have an up to date list of media you can contact as well as

---

[390] Kinzey, 100-102.

[391] Kinzey, 17.

[392] Kinzey, 91.

[393] Kinzey, 92.

[394] Shannon, "How to create a crisis communications plan for your nonprofit organization".

[395] Kinzey, 86.

[396] Kinzey, 87.

[397] Kinzey, 86.

organizations you can collaborate with and people you can mobilize.[398] Think about who would have a stake in any given crisis scenario.[399] In particular, it is important to know people independent from your organization who will be prepared to speak out on behalf of it.[400] It may also be helpful to ensure key people have media training.[401]

You could also practice crisis simulations with your team regularly.[402] There are agencies that specialize in these simulations.[403]

During Crisis: Holding Statement, Gather Info, Update

Even if you have prepared messages, you always want your response to be as tailored to the specific facts of the situation as possible. However, you will not have all the information you need right away in order to do that and you should not rush to respond.[404] Consequently, your first step during a crisis is to post a "holding statement" on all your platforms (especially those where the story broke).[405] A holding statement informs the audience that you are aware of the situation and are monitoring it closely and they should expect an update from you soon.[406] If possible, you want to be the one to bring the issue to the attention of the media and not the other way around.[407]

Once you have posted the holding statement, you should then start gathering information so you really understand the situation before

---

[398] Kinzey, 93.

[399] Davis, "How to Handle Crisis Communication," 7.

[400] Davis, "How to Handle Crisis Communication"; Nonprofit Risk Management, "Communicating During a Crisis".

[401] Colorado Nonprofit Association, "Crisis Communication Plan Nonprofit Toolkit," 9.

[402] Kinzey, 85.

[403] Shannon, "How to create a crisis communications plan for your nonprofit organization".

[404] Shannon, "How to create a crisis communications plan for your nonprofit organization".

[405] Kinzey, 96; Shannon, "How to create a crisis communications plan for your nonprofit organization".

[406] Nonprofit Communications Report, "Five Tips for Communicating Through a Crisis," 14 No 8 (July 20, 2016): 3.

[407] Nonprofit Communications Report, "Five Tips for Communicating Through Crisis".

you publish something more specific.[408] Listen to what journalists, other organizations, and individuals are saying about the crisis.[409] It is very important to listen for misinformation and to correct it as early as possible.[410] Ultimately, you want to do everything possible to ensure your messages to the public are consistent and timely.[411] You also want your messages to be reassuring to the public by taking responsibility, forgetting about blame, and being transparent.[412] Finally, it is good for your messages to be action-oriented.[413]

Accomplishing the above goals requires strong internal communication as well as external,[414] including regular check-ins both inside and outside your organization.[415] In sum, monitoring should be ongoing, and you should be prepared to adapt to changes.[416] You never want to disappear from the evolving conversations on any of your platforms.[417]

Lastly, while crises may be fast-paced and stressful, you should remain calm and take care of yourself.[418] You should also consider continuing business as usual to the greatest extent possible in order to show strength in the face of adversity.[419] Furthermore, you should never lose sight of the fact that even in a crisis your communications must align with your overall mission.[420]

---

[408] Kinzey, 97; Geller, "Four Tips for Navigating a Crisis," *Nonprofit Communications Report*, 17 No 1 (December 10, 2018): 4.

[409] Kinzey, 103; Susan Raymond, *Recession, Recovery and Renewal*. (Hoboken, NJ: John Wiley & Sons, Inc., 2019), 214-15.

[410] Kinzey, 104; "Crisis Communication Plan Nonprofit Toolkit", 7.

[411] Kinzey, 109.

[412] Shannon, "How to create a crisis communications plan for your nonprofit organization".

[413] Colorado Nonprofit Association, "Crisis Communication Plan Nonprofit Toolkit".

[414] Corrine Geller, "Four Tips for Navigating a Crisis", *Nonprofit Communications Report*, 17 No 1 (December 10, 2018): 4.

[415] Morand, "How to Create a Crisis Communications Plan for Your Nonprofit", Nonprofit Risk Management Center.

[416] Davis, "How to Handle Crisis Communication".

[417] Morand, "How to Create a Crisis Communications Plan for Your Nonprofit".

[418] Geller, "Four Tips for Navigating a Crisis", *Nonprofit Communications Report*.

[419] Lisa McCale, "Show Grace Under Pressure During a Crisis Nonprofit," *Progressive Women's Leadership* (August 2, 2016).

[420] Melinda Beckett-Maines, "Strategies to Up Your Crisis Management Game," *Nonprofit Communications Report*, (January 2019).

Post Crisis: Debriefing and Measuring Return to Normal

After the crisis, you should take stock of how the crisis was handled, as well as how to keep it from happening again.[421] This is a good time to recognize heroes and update your crisis communication plan in light of what worked.[422]

Furthermore, you should measure your recovery.[423] Often the assumed metric is whether you get "back to normal", measured in terms of your organization's operations, finances, and management.[424] "When it comes right down to it, crisis communications are all about the strategic way you can restore and preserve your organization's reputation."[425]

However, you must also be mindful that the effect of many crises is difficult to discern.[426] Issues such as racial hatred or reconciliation may come to a head in a given moment but the long-term fall-out of that moment is unclear. Regardless, you should continue to act on a crisis even after it is officially declared "over".[427]

THE PROBLEM: YOU MAY NEED CRISIS

While the types of crises above are important, and the practical tools are useful for other types of crisis, we will be talking about a different kind of crisis. I will use the term crisis for those events Skinner portrays as moments in which individuals, institutions, and societies redefine their moral identity through conflict that forces them to make a choice about the meaning of keywords. Crucially, however, Skinner teaches us that these moments can only be understood

---

[421] Morand, "How to Create a Crisis Communications Plan for Your Nonprofit"; Colorado Nonprofit Association, "Crisis Communication Plan Nonprofit Toolkit".

[422] Colorado Nonprofit Association, "Crisis Communication Plan Nonprofit Toolkit," 12.

[423] Kinzey, 114.

[424] Raymond, *Recession, Recovery and Renewal*, 215; Tricia Ann Jordan, Paula Upright, Kristeen Tice-Owens, "Crisis Management in Nonprofit Organizations A Case Study of Crisis Communication and Planning," *Journal of Nonprofit Education and Leadership* 6 No 2 (2016): 159–177.

[425] Meg Shannon, "How to create a crisis communications plan for your nonprofit organization". Nonprofit Mar Community (December 3, 2015).

[426] Raymond, 214-15.

[427] Kinzey, 110.

through the decades and centuries that both preceded and followed these moments. We will see what movements in the past did that allowed them to succeed when the moment was right and carry the momentary gain into long-term transformation afterwards.

Above all, I hope you take away that if you want to be a successful innovating ideologist, these kinds of crises are often necessary. Consequently, successful crisis communication is not just about prevention and mitigation and getting back to normal. Rather, it is about encouraging the right crisis, getting the most out of it and ensuring things do not go back to normal.

Defining Crisis: Forcing the Question

Societies in which people radically disagree are only possible because moral languages are capable of containing contradictions. Those interested in maintaining the status quo will therefore have to find practical compromises, de-emphasize the importance of these conflicts, and define words in ways that allow potentially conflicting words to be compatible.

For example, in the early 1600s, the King of England insisted that Parliament was ultimately beholden to his "royal prerogative" (i.e., he could do whatever he wanted and had the ultimate veto).[428] Parliamentarians insisted that for Englishmen to be free they could not be subject to anyone's arbitrary rule. Royalists, however, argued that the King would never use his prerogative except for the benefit and protection of Englishmen and therefore of course they were free. A tension therefore existed for decades between the division of powers between the King and Parliament, and different ideas about liberty. Still, for a long time the country managed to function.

A crisis in legitimacy happens when circumstances lay bare an underlying tension in the dominant moral language and force the decision-maker to make a choice between the competing meanings of keywords. This often happens when institutions fail for some material reason that prevents them from being able to placate all parties (e.g., economic crisis, war, famine, natural disaster, etc.).

For example, Skinner argued that the timing of the start of the English Civil War can be explained by the decades-long simmering

---

[428] Skinner, *From Humanism to Hobbes*, 143.

debate over the relationship of liberty to the royal prerogative. This conflict was only worsened by the King's increasing financial demands on Parliament, driven by the King's failed policies. In 1642, Parliament prepared to pass a law that would put the military under its control. The King then said he would veto any such law, thereby putting the prerogative in issue.[429] Parliament went ahead anyway without his approval thus forcing a fundamental choice for society about whether the King had any distinctive lawmaking power. The King refused to change his position. The result was a civil war.

A civil war came about because neither position was capable of rallying enough support to its side at the outset to push past opposition or scare it into submission. It is this inability to raise sufficient support that makes it a crisis in legitimacy. Resolving the crisis of legitimacy means either rallying enough support to one course of action or depleting the opposition to it, so that it is possible to move ahead. In the worst-case scenario this is done by coercion, but it is also done through persuasion and dissuasion (e.g., protests can make a decision politically costly or embarrassing). In the process of resolving the relationship of liberty to the royal prerogative, i.e., deciding ultimately what role the King would play in law-making, the decision-maker and sometimes whole societies are transformed in this way.[430]

I don't want you to think the process I just described is reserved for grand historical events. The same process Skinner describes can also be applied to "micro" or personal crises. The stages are:

1. Simmering tension fed by innovating ideologists and a material breakdown

2. Event that provokes a choice between the competing meaning of the words

3. Dissident's refusal to let business carry on as usual when the prevalent meaning is employed

4. Decision-maker's refusal to back down from the decision

5. Insufficient support for the decision to proceed as normal

6. Conflict

[429] Skinner, *From Humanism to Hobbes*, 147.
[430] Skinner, *Meaning & Context*, 112.

7. Either the old norm is re-established at a cost or a new bargain is struck.

Take for example, campaigns such as #itjustgotweird by the Ottawa Coalition to End Violence Against Women.[431] These campaigns are designed to encourage people to speak up when men engage in those behaviours that society tolerates as "weird" but does not regard as "violent".

1. **The simmering tension**: increasing discomfort with sexist jokes (debating the meaning of "funny")

2. **An event that provokes a choice**: someone tells a sexist joke

3. **A dissident refuses**: Someone calls out the joke teller and refuses to let the conversation proceed until the situation is resolved, e.g., the joke teller apologizes.

4. **A decision-maker refuses**: The joke teller insists it was "just a joke".

5. **Insufficient support**: There are a variety of opinions in the group of friends.

6. **Conflict**: Argument ensues, perhaps people are cold to one another over time, etc.

7. **Renormalization**: The sexist jokes keep getting told perhaps at the cost of a friendship or sexist jokes stop getting told, or they are only told in the presence of some, etc.

Nonprofits, communities, and movements create different kinds of crises in a variety of ways, such as erecting blockades to pipelines, refusing to wear masks, occupying public parks, etc. Events may also happen that similarly force choices (e.g., mass deaths in long-term care homes) without anyone consciously bringing them about. The lesson is that nonprofits can and do harness the power of crises of legitimacy to force questions on individuals, institutions, and society. Crisis communications should not only, or even primarily, be about prevention and mitigation, but be about effectively pressing these choices to encourage the innovations you seek.

---

[431] Ottawa Coalition to End Violence Against Women, "It Just Got Weird" http://justgotweird.com/.

Pre-Crisis: Stewarding Ideas, Preparing for Tough Questions

As I mentioned, Skinner does not see these moments as spontaneous events. They are the boiling over of decades and sometimes centuries of simmering tensions.[432] Phase 1 of the crisis as I described it above clearly shows that nonprofits must build support for a position some time before a crisis is even possible (otherwise why would anyone insist on the issue?).[433] Even if you get no traction over decades, cultivating a sense that there is a problem, or cultivating a solution to a problem so it is at the decision-maker's finger tips when they need it, is one of the most important ways you can prepare for a crisis.

Skinner also observes how the choices of movements made them particularly vulnerable to certain kinds of crisis. For example, for decades, Luther and other leading Lutherans preached total non-resistance to state authorities. In 1543, Charles V moved his forces down the Rhine in preparation for a holy war on Protestants.[434] This aggressive act forced Lutherans into a choice between their ongoing commitment to survival and their theological commitment to non-resistance to the government.[435] They did manage to develop theological-legal justifications for resistance, but it took valuable time to develop and build internal consensus. Ultimately, external conditions distracted Charles V and a massacre was avoided, but had it not been, Lutherans would have been caught at a serious disadvantage.

Nonprofits also need to be mindful of how their communications and commitments might restrict them, be used against them, or limit their ability to act when a crisis in legitimacy is forced. This happens when nonprofits argue for social benefits on the grounds that individuals will use it productively as opposed to, for example, on the basis of human rights. Individual stories of frivolous use will necessarily put supporters of the social benefit on the defensive. Had the basis been more rights oriented, examples of individual frivolous use would have less force (e.g., it would be possible to respond, "We refuse to be paternalistic. It was never about their use but their right."). When crafting

---

[432] Skinner, *The Foundations of Modern Political Thought*, 71.

[433] Skinner, *The Foundations of Modern Political Thought*, 149.

[434] Skinner, *The Foundations of Modern Political Thought Volume 2*, 189-191.

[435] Skinner, 191, 194.

justifications and communications strategies, therefore, nonprofits must be mindful of how these justifications could hinder them in a pinch.

During Crisis: Building Consensus to Move Forward

In a reputational crisis, a nonprofit can resolve the crisis by sending messages that preserve the public's trust in the nonprofit. This means being clear, consistent, and adapting to the facts. In a crisis of legitimacy, resolution means building a critical mass of support or undermining opposition sufficiently for a decision-maker to proceed with one course of action over another.

Skinner shows how understanding the ideological landscape will tell you which solutions will be capable of building sufficient support in a crisis to create a coalition that is capable of moving forward. For example, during the English Civil War, there were different factions among Parliamentarians. They disagreed about, among other things, who should have the vote in the new English Republic.[436] Skinner argues that the compromise that was eventually achieved can best be understood by understanding how liberty was defined for the Parliamentarians.

Being able to offer a decision-maker in crisis a solution that you have spent decades building a consensus around will make it much easier for them to move forward quickly.

Post-Crisis: Finding a New Normal

Often, advisors seem to implicitly see the goal of crisis communication as getting you back to normal. For the innovating ideologist, returning to the previous normal means either:

- a categorical failure, if they were hoping to make gains, or
- a stalemate if the crisis threatened the meaning of their important terms in the existing moral vocabulary.

However, I think it is right to observe that a nonprofit has only confirmed their success once a state of normalcy has been reached. For example, a nonprofit may mobilize many during an oil spill to prevent significant harm to an ocean ecosystem, yet after the fact it is still

---

[436] Skinner, *The Foundations of Modern Political Thought Volume 2*, 158.

slowly destroyed through incremental pollution. The prioritization of protecting ocean ecosystems was not successfully normalized.

During a crisis, it may be tempting to mobilize people primarily to meet the immediate need. However, if one does not mobilize people in a long-term way during the moment of crisis when support for their innovation might be highest, an opportunity will be wasted, and at best all one might have done is preserve the status quo. I do not mean to belittle such an accomplishment. Especially in the face of a crisis, worlds must be actively cared for to be maintained. Nevertheless, crisis communications can contribute to your ultimate goal of innovation if you see the long-term potential in the moment.

THE SOLUTION: PLAN FOR CRISIS

The phases of crisis that we observed provides us with a model for transformative crisis communications.

1. **The simmering tension**: This phase reflects the work all the previous chapters of the book should help you plan for. Your work should be building this tension especially among your silent opposition. It doesn't need to be part of your crisis plan.

2. **An event that provokes a choice**: To plan for this phase, bring a team together to brainstorm decisions in which the decision-maker will be forced to choose between two conflicting commitments in the existing moral language. You will want to prioritize based on frequency or stakes, controllability, the extent to which it will cast your meaning of the keyword in a sympathetic light, and whether you will be able to maintain sufficient support to persist through the crisis.

3. **A dissident refuses**: For each high-priority choice identified in Step 2, you will want to identify who is capable of preventing the choice from proceeding business as usual and how they could prevent the choice from being made.

4. **A decision-maker refuses**: You should prepare to respond to the decision-maker's arguments should they choose to push forward business as usual.

5. **Insufficient support**: In Chapter 7, you identified potential allies. In this part of the plan, you will think about how you

would mobilize those allies in the specific situation of this crisis. It is most important to mobilize those allies whose support the decision-maker needs to move ahead.

6. **Conflict**: This is the logistical part of the plan and should basically reflect the traditional crisis communication plan in which you clearly assign roles, develop materials, etc. You will also want to think about what steps you can take to legitimize the actions your supporters will need to take to effectively participate.

7. **Renormalization**: In this stage you will think about what new norm could come out of the crisis and what action is needed to cement it. You will want to think about how to mobilize people during the crisis towards these long-term actions.

An Event That Provokes a Choice: Choosing the Right Crisis

You should not jump on every crisis and try to make it about your issue. You should limit your brainstorming to choices that the decision-maker must make identified in Chapter 5, in which the choices available raise a trade-off between the two keywords in the moral vocabulary you identified as ripe for innovation. It is likely that the decision-maker makes choices every day that raise this conflict. The more polarized the choice, the easier it will be for you to frame the decision. A physical choice, e.g., put in or do not put in the pipeline, often offers the best catalyst for making an otherwise complex social conflict tangible for people. You can prioritize which choices to target by focusing on frequency or stakes, controllability, and how sympathetic a light it casts your innovation in.

Firstly, you will want to target either relatively low stakes choices that are very frequent (e.g., like the sexist joke) or high-stakes choices that are less frequent (e.g., a significant piece of legislation in your area).

If you opt for the frequency strategy, you are essentially aiming for a bottom-up approach to social crisis that, if it achieves a critical mass, could collectively trigger a collective crisis, such as #MeToo (e.g., individual accusations add up to such an extent that most employers are forced to reassess their policies).

If you opt for a focus on high-stakes, infrequent choices, then you will naturally face greater competition and more barriers to participation, but if you are successful in affecting the outcome, its direct effect may be greater, and others will be more likely to look to it as a precedent. If you can combine both, such as a high-stakes but frequent choice (e.g., refusing a refugee claim) then you are in the best position.

Secondly, choices where you have greater opportunity to intervene are a necessary precondition to being able to escalate a "non-issue" into a crisis. For example, we saw in Chapter 5 how although many people were opposed to making the Canadian long form census voluntary, institutionally, no one could do anything about it, so the choice went ahead despite opposition.

Thirdly, the circumstances of the choice must be such as to make your proposed innovation more sympathetic. For example, suppose you are advocating for alternative electoral system on the grounds that it is more "democratic". You will be disadvantaged if you push, for example, for a referendum, at a time when there is a political party that many find dangerous or offensive but that nonetheless enjoys sufficient support under your proposed innovation to enter the legislature. The principle may be no different from your perspective, but the circumstances will affect others support of your proposal.

Selecting a Target Crisis Worksheet

Choice	Keywords in tension	Frequency	Stakes	Ability to intervene	How it paints your innovation	Notes

A "Dissident" Refuses: Disrupting Business as Usual

In a democratic society, most choices can be disrupted by someone. For the choice or choices you identified above, identify who, if they so choose, could disrupt the business as usual. It could be because of their physical presence on the scene. It could be because their approval is needed before the decision can move ahead. In any case, you must identify these individuals as well as what could motivate them to persist in not allowing business to proceed as usual.

For some, their opposition will come at a personal cost to themselves. For example, if they are a protester, it will take time and resources and have a financial cost if they must travel or take time away from work. If they are a politician, it may take political capital. Incentivizing means not only winning them over to your cause but covering, compensating or at least recognizing that cost so that at the very least it is logistically possible for them to maintain the opposition.

For others, their opposition will be insulated from costs. The best example of this in Canadian society is the Court. For these types of actors, there will be an institutionally mandated way to secure their opposition, e.g., you will have to show how the existing law requires the court to approve an injunction.

Mapping out all the decision points that lead to the choice you identified above will give you all the potential veto points. How you choose to press a crisis will shape that crisis. For example, if protesters insist what they are doing is legal, then it becomes a crisis about what the law is. If they say they acknowledge it is illegal but nonetheless just, it becomes a crisis of the legitimacy of extra-judicial action (or the need to change the law).

Understanding what tensions in the existing moral language are holding your mission back will tell you precisely what the nature of the crisis will need to be in order for its resolution to be a potentially significant step in your favour. This will inform which "dissident" (official or unofficial) is best positioned to represent your innovation and how their opposition should manifest.

A Decision-Maker Refuses: Preparing for the Pushback

Once opposition has been raised, the decision-maker has the option to retract or change their choice. If they do, you have not yet reached a crisis. If the decision-maker concedes the point at this point, it may be a good sign that your innovation is incrementally gaining ground, but this will not necessarily be the transformative moment of a crisis.

If the decision-maker refuses to back down, then you have reached an impasse, business as usual has been disrupted and to a greater or lesser extent a "crisis" has begun. The decision-maker will inevitably have justifications for their decision not to back down. After all, if their decision represented business as usual, there will generally be some reason a sufficient coalition of interests has supported the choice until now. Furthermore, there will be an automatic prejudice against the one who disrupts business as usual, if only because they are "holding things up". Imagine what these arguments will be and be prepared to answer them.

Insufficient Support: Mobilizing Allies

During a crisis, it is all about changing the balance of support and opposition for one course of action or another. It is important to understand how the decision-maker thinks (see Chapter 5) in order to understand what coalition of interests will be needed to change their calculation. That is why it is so important not only to mobilize your allies but to create change among the individuals and institutions who form the silent opposition. Often the silent opposition will also represent the source of support on which the decision-maker depends, and therefore your ability to mobilize people and institutions outside of this silent opposition may never be sufficient to sway the decision-maker (though, as I have said, it may serve as the source for alternative institutions).

Conflict: Organizing Logistics and Justifying the Means

It is obviously good advice to have a clear division of labour during a crisis and consistent but adapting messages. I will not contradict that. In the subsection above I discussed very different types of crises, ranging from war to awkward situations. At this point, I want to discuss a point I alluded to at the beginning of this book: words are never enough.

As we have discussed, words are powerful because they can legitimize or delegitimize different kinds of action, but it is ultimately the actions people are willing or not willing to take and stick to that will create the crisis and resolve it. In the English Civil War, that meant being so committed to a certain sense of the word "liberty" and the authority of Parliament that you were willing to fight and die for it. In the case of the sexist joke that meant being willing to speak up and possibly lose friends over it.

On one level, nonprofit communications advice clearly understands this. After all, you are told over and over again to make your messages "action-oriented". Advisors have to speak to a wide range of nonprofits, but they usually have a few types of action in mind: donating, volunteering, attending an event, sharing something on social media, calling your MP, or signing a petition.

I would only add to this that you need to understand the nature of how the crisis will be resolved and must spend time to not only justify your goals, but also the means you have identified as necessary to achieve those goals. This connects back to what I said earlier about what a decision-maker believes about their role. Your audience may believe in your objective, but not believe that doing what you see as necessary is legitimate. They may also simply be unwilling to do it.

Renormalization: Getting Back to a New Normal

As I mentioned earlier in this chapter, the goal for the innovating ideologist is achieving a normal, but it's a new normal, not the old one.

As I have mentioned before, pluralistic societies depend on being able to paper over radical conflicts. The papering over will always be to the advantage of one view or another. Nevertheless, it is in most people's interests to have a functioning society rather than constant conflict. If it is not in someone's interest, their ability to sustain such a conflict may still be limited. Consequently, as long as the compromise manages to more or less sustain people, the terms of this compromise will be accepted. That means that once people's resources run out there will be a tendency, even among your supporters, to rush to the least disruptive compromise that satisfies the conflicting commitments somewhat.

In order for you to ensure that "least disruptive compromise" is a norm different from the one you left, it is incumbent on you to develop the laws, institutional mechanisms, and in some case technologies that make it as easy and cheap as possible for the decision-maker to transition to the innovated moral vocabulary you are proposing.

Chapter 10

You May Not Get Value for Money

"A policeman sees a drunk man searching for something under a streetlight and asks what the drunk has lost. He says he lost his keys and they both look under the streetlight together. After a few minutes the policeman asks if he is sure he lost them here, and the drunk replies, no, and that he lost them in the park. The policeman asks why he is searching here, and the drunk replies, 'This is where the light is.'"

Evaluation has become increasingly important in all aspects of a nonprofit's work. In this chapter, I will look at some conventional wisdom on evaluating nonprofit communications and why it has difficulty capturing long-term ideological transformation. I will close by suggesting how existing evaluation practices could be adapted to better suit long-term ideological change.

In this chapter you will learn:

- The limits of evaluation in long-term ideological change
- One possible method for evaluating long-term ideological change.

CONVENTIONAL WISDOM ON EVALUATION

The Value of Evaluation: Accountability and Effectiveness

Evaluation is a vital part of communications and should be conducted throughout. It should be planned with the design of the project.[437] The two main purposes of evaluation are to prove the value of your work to donors and funders, and to improve on the work you are doing by spotting errors and environmental changes so you can change course.[438] The values underlying these two goals are accountability and effectiveness.[439] Because there are different possible goals, it is important to clarify from the outset who your audience for this evaluation will be (external or internal).[440]

Demonstrating Value for Money to Donors and Funders

Because donors no longer trust nonprofits and more nonprofits are competing for funds, donors and funders increasingly demand to see value for money and in particular visual evidence of impact (seeing is believing!).[441] This desire is compounded by social media, which leads people to expect constant updates in the form of multimedia content.[442] In short, you want to be able to tell uplifting stories about the difference your work is making to inspire donors.[443]

In a different way, this short-term focus is encouraged by government grants that have to be renewed every year and are tied to election commitments that must be delivered on by the next election.[444] In

[437] SaskCulture, "The Communications Plan"; Communications Consortium Media Center, "Guidelines for Evaluating Nonprofit Communications Efforts," CCMC (April 2004): 2.
[438] Communications Consortium Media Center, "Guidelines for Evaluating Nonprofit Communications Efforts".
[439] Diane Ell, "Evaluation of Communications," SaskCulture (2020).
[440] Communications Consortium Media Center, "Guidelines for Evaluating Nonprofit Communications Efforts," 2.
[441] Kinzey, *Promoting nonprofit organizations*, 4; Wiggill, *Strategic communication management*, 226; Patterson and Radtke, *Strategic Communications*, 151; Hager and Searing, "10 Ways to Kill Your Nonprofit".
[442] Kinzey, 4.
[443] Azelrad, "The 9 Signs of a Successful Social Media Strategy for Nonprofits".
[444] Brinckerhoff, *Mission-based marketing*, 5.

some cases, nonprofits may have to demonstrate their impact in hundreds of reports a year.[445]

In all cases, do not make promises of results you cannot possibly fulfill.[446] This may sound obvious, but I mention it because we will come back to it when we talk about how this limits your ambitions.

Learning for Course Corrections

The other major purpose of evaluation is to determine what is and isn't working, or what has changed, so that you can adjust your strategies.[447] You must even be prepared to quickly terminate your plan altogether.[448] As some have said "measure and evaluate. Then measure and evaluate again." because the best nonprofits rely on data to adjust strategies and ensure ongoing accountability.[449]

Adapting Your Evaluation to Your Theory of Change

There is no "right" or "wrong" way to evaluate, since everything depends on what you are trying to accomplish.[450] Furthermore, there are no widely accepted guidelines.[451] The most important thing to define therefore is how you will get from your activities to your goals.

Defining Your Theory of Change

Your evaluation strategy should be based around your "theory of change".[452] A theory of change is your (ideally research-based) prediction of how your activities will create the conditions where it will be

---

[445] L. Eakin, "We Can't Afford to do Business This Way: A Study of the Administrative Burden Resulting From Funder Accountability and Compliance Practices," Wellesley Institute.

[446] Communications Consortium Media Center, "Guidelines for Evaluating Nonprofit Communications Efforts".

[447] Kinzey, 20; Patterson & Radtke, *Strategic Communications.*

[448] Kinzey, 46.

[449] Walker, "Solving the World's Biggest Problems".

[450] Communications Consortium Media Center, "Guidelines for Evaluating Nonprofit Communications Efforts," 2.

[451] Communications Consortium Media Center, "Guidelines for Evaluating Nonprofit Communications Efforts," 3-4.

[452] Communications Consortium Media Center, "Guidelines for Evaluating Nonprofit Communications Efforts," 3, 6.

possible for the change you are aiming for to happen. You can map it out visually by including: your activities, short-term outcomes, intermediate outcomes, and ultimate purpose.[453]

Texts on evaluation sometimes suggest specific theories of change for you to follow. For example, one guide states that changing governmental policy usually follows this path "awareness, building champions/supporters, constituency building, public will, policy goal".[454] That same guide suggests that behavioural change follows this path:

- The individual becomes aware of the issue,
- The issue becomes increasingly salient for the individual,
- The individual changes their attitudes and beliefs about the issue,
- Their ability to act improves,
- Social norms change,
- The individual forms an intention to act, and
- The individual's behaviour changes.[455]

You should take these broad theories of change and tailor them to your specific path. Each step will then inform what you track.

What to Track

The more precise your theory of change the more limited the scope will be of relevant data to which you have to pay attention.[456] Some examples of what to track include: shifts in public opinion, policy changes, increased memberships and organizational participation, and improved institutional capacity.[457]

---

[453] Communications Consortium Media Center, "Guidelines for Evaluating Nonprofit Communications Efforts," 9.

[454] Asibey Consulting, "Keeping People Engaged in Your Cause With Help From Behavioural Science," (2019): 7-8.

[455] Asibey Consulting, 8-9.

[456] Kinzey, 52.

[457] Kathy Bonk, Emily Tynes, Henry Griggs, Phil Sparks, "Strategic Communications for Nonprofits. A Step-by-Step Guide to Working With the Media, 2nd ed," (San Francisco: Jossey-Bass A Wiley Imprint, 2008): 28.

Whatever your theory of change, you should start by establishing a baseline.[458] This means capturing your starting point, for example current participation in your events, common misperceptions, current news coverage, etc.[459] Success will be measured against this baseline, so it is really important to make it relevant.

In order to determine what information to capture, consider what you are trying to change. If you are trying to change individual behaviour, individuals will be your unit of analysis.[460] If you are trying to change the culture of a community or country, then those will be your units of analysis. You will then want data that is relevant to what you are trying to change.

Setting Goals/Objectives for Yourself

The next step according to the conventional wisdom is to break down your theory of change into ultimate goals and the corresponding objectives, or milestones along the way. These specific, measurable and achievable milestones will be what you evaluate.[461]

Setting Goals

Ultimately, you're trying to change something in the world. Your goals correspond to this ultimate outcome.[462] A goal is the long-term change that you want to bring about.[463] Writing on evaluation tends to offer a spectrum of goals ranging from changing individual behaviour to changing government policy.[464] We already spoke in Chapter 3 about how this way of goal setting is limited, but the focus in the evaluation literature I reviewed is on objectives anyway.

---

[458] Upleaf Technology Solutions; Social Media Group, "Going Social"; Asibey Consulting, 15.

[459] Ell, "Evaluation of Communications".

[460] Communications Consortium Media Center, "Guidelines for Evaluating Nonprofit Communications Efforts", 8.

[461] Patterson and Radtke, *"Strategic Communications,"* 151-152.

[462] "What are strategic communications?" IDEA .org.

[463] Asibey Consulting, 6.

[464] Asibey Consulting, 7.

SMART Objectives

It's not really the goals you evaluate but the objectives.[465] Objectives are measurable statements that represent attainable outcomes.[466] Objectives are different from goals in that they are measurable, shorter-term (e.g., 1-2 years) milestones on the way to your ultimate goal.[467]

The advice is often to formulate your objectives according to the SMART formula.[468] This means they must be specific, measurable, achievable, realistic, and time-bound.[469] SMART objectives should tell you if you are closer to your goal.[470]

"Specific" means that you must be able to specify who will be affected and how they will be affected in terms of their behaviour, knowledge, or attitude.[471] The more specific, the easier it will be to measure, and much advice strongly encourages as much measurement as possible.[472]

Measuring impact is an intermediate step before the outcome you are ultimately trying to accomplish. The longer term your communications plan the more important it is to have intermediate objectives to attain at reasonable intervals (e.g., 6 months to 1 year).[473] Establishing which measurements is crucial to knowing if you're succeeding or not.[474] In the social media context, this means asking what the pinnacle of engagement from your user is, e.g., conversions to donations, volunteering, etc.[475]

There is some acknowledgement that many goals cannot be adequately measured because we do not understand them or they are out of our control (e.g., eliminating hatred, achieving artistic

---

[465] CallHub, "4 Steps For An Effective Nonprofit Communications Strategy".

[466] Kinzey, 36.

[467] Asibey Consulting, 11.

[468] Asibey Consulting, 12.

[469] Patterson and Radtke, 153.

[470] Ell, "Evaluation of Communications".

[471] Patterson and Radtke, 154.

[472] Williams, *Marketing & Communications*.

[473] Upleaf Technology Solutions, "Nonprofit communications plan template"; Raymond, *Recession, Recovery and Renewal*, 216.

[474] Social Media Group, "Going Social"; Raymond, *Recession, Recovery and Renewal*, 215.

[475] Lee, "Social Media for Non-Profits".

excellence).[476] Nevertheless, even those who acknowledge this concede that the need for accountability to funders requires that decisions still be evidence-based.[477] They therefore recommend focusing on the efficiency of internal processes.

Tracking Progress

There are different types of evaluation that are appropriate to different stages of your campaign and serve different goals within it. How you track the above-mentioned objectives will depend on what type of evaluation you are doing. You may be doing:

- Prospective evaluation of the quality of materials
- Process-oriented evaluation of how efficiently you are communicating
- Impact-oriented evaluation to see what effect your communications is having on your audience
- Outcome-oriented evaluation to see what effect your communications is having on the world.[478]

In all types of evaluation, you should strive for methodological rigour, mixed methods, and an understanding the limits of the methods you use.[479] You are always asking yourself "What questions will tell me if I am moving closer to my goals?"[480] The answers should reveal the strengths and weaknesses of your campaign at any given point.[481]

Below, I will consider each type of evaluation in a bit more detail.

Prospective Evaluation

Prospective evaluation is about testing out your materials with your target audiences before releasing them to the public. It can be

---

[476] Raymond, 214-15.

[477] Raymond, 215.

[478] Bonk, *Strategic Communications for Nonprofits*, 153; Communications Consortium Media Center, "Guidelines for Evaluating Nonprofit Communications Efforts," 10-13.

[479] Communications Consortium Media Center, "Guidelines for Evaluating Nonprofit Communications Efforts," 2-3.

[480] Ell, "Evaluation of Communications".

[481] Asibey Consulting, 17.

especially helpful in deciding what mediums to use.[482] For example, you can present a tweet, a Facebook post, and a blog article to a focus group and see how they react to each in order to determine which is the best format for that message.

Prospective evaluation is most important early in campaigns. Early on, you may be engaged in a lot of trial and error, and prospective evaluations will help you identify strategic directions and sharpen your approach.[483]

Process Evaluation

The simplest way to evaluate your process is to evaluate the quantity of your activities/outputs, e.g., articles, events, reports, tweets, etc. and what it takes you to produce these.[484] For example, you should keep track of how much time and resources it takes you to produce various outputs, e.g., articles, events, etc.[485] In general, you are measuring inputs and outputs.

Impact Evaluation

Impact evaluation should be focused on a sample that reflects the audience you are trying to reach.[486] This may include tracking who has received and acted on your message, e.g., by supporting your cause.[487] To gauge impact, you may use methods such as surveys, interviews, focus groups, observation, content analysis, and usage tracking.[488] This is an important kind of evaluation mid-course to make sure you are on track.[489]

Outcome Evaluation

It is pretty much universally recognized that it is difficult to measure the impact your communication has had on society, since there are

---

[482] SaskCulture, "Communications for Non-Profits".

[483] Asibey Consulting, 16.

[484] Patterson and Radtke, *Strategic Communications*, 154.

[485] Ell, "Evaluation of Communications".

[486] Asibey Consulting, 13.

[487] Patterson and Radtke, 154-55.

[488] Ell, "Evaluation of Communications".

[489] Asibey Consulting, 19.

YOU MAY NOT GET VALUE FOR MONEY

inevitably complex forces at work behind every development.[490] Nevertheless, you should strive to determine what actual change has happened in the world.

THE PROBLEM: THE SLOW, CONFUSING, AND UNPREDICTABLE MARCH OF HISTORY

In this part, I will consider how the "value for money" paradigm is likely inappropriate for the 100-year PR Plan, so that evaluation is mainly about internal learning. Secondly, I will suggest that Skinner's theories offer us a basic model for our theory of change. Finally, I will discuss the gulf between an ideologically transformative goal and SMART objectives.

The Value of Evaluation

In this section I will discuss the many reasons to be hesitant about using evaluation as a tool to show the "value for money" of ideologically transformative work. In particular, I will focus on how "efficiency" can only really show value for money where your strategy depends on mass production rather than the creation of high-quality original work. On the other hand, it is vital for you to constantly be evaluating your landscape to see what effect you are having and how it has changed in order to determine whether you are working with the same language as when you started.

Indicators of Value for Money are Largely False Certainty

The tension between long-term ideological change and the pressure to demonstrate value for money to donors and funders comes at many levels.

Firstly, in Chapter 4, we saw why, when it comes to ideological transformation, you cannot simply give the customer what they want. The same is true when it comes to evaluation. The donor or funder may not see what you are trying to achieve as valuable and that is precisely part of the problem. If you have ever had to "tone down" a report so it does not alienate your constituencies, you will know what I mean.

---

[490] Patterson and Radtke, 155.

Secondly, if you think of evaluation this way, then you are treating your evaluation as just another arm of your communications campaign. It is unclear how doing that encourages accountability. If anything, it encourages the opposite. As we explored in Chapter 3, what is good for the organization is not necessarily good for the mission, and vice versa.

Thirdly, on the face of it, the nature of long-term ideological shift simply does not lend itself to regularly sharing images that provide a satisfying and simple story of success. One exception to this may be where part of your ideological innovation is to press the import-ance of certain metrics (such as ecological footprint) or graphs (such as income concentration in the top 1% of earners). Providing regular updates on this will cement them as the relevant measures in the minds of your audience even if you consistently report failure. Beware of graphs though! As I will explain, quantifying ideological change is an inherently fraught activity.

Fourthly, you might say that even if you cannot measure your goal, surely you can turn inwards and at least show value for money in the efficiency of your process. Sometimes you can and sometimes you can't. Efficiency only works as a metric for ideological transforma-tion strategies that depend on the output of an agreed upon message, rather than the production of justifications of that message.

Recall back in Chapter 6 we talked about two kinds of communi-cation products: high-quality long format products that explicitly justify your linguistic innovation, and products that propagate the innovation by using it. If you are producing the former, then I think the lesson from Skinner's studies of great works like Machiavelli's *The Prince* and Hobbes' *Leviathan*, is that a thousand books which just reproduce the moral language of the day do not replace one that sharply subverts it in novel ways. As the story goes, Karl Marx took 10 years to write the last chapter of *Das Kapital*. Indeed, if his publisher had been a nonprofit, think of the outcry among donors and funders. But the rest, as they say, is history. If the strategy you choose is to produce long-format high quality materials, efficiency may be an almost meaningless if not counter-productive indicator.

I should not be taken as making excuses for wasteful practices. My point is rather that you cannot escape fraught qualitative questions.

You may have turned to efficiency because you wanted a nice neutral measure to reassure your donors in a confusing world where you are striving for an intangible goal. But efficiency, in many cases, provides a false sense of certainty.

When is efficiency relevant as an indicator for showing value for money in ideologically transformative work? It seems to me efficiency only makes sense if your strategy truly relies on simply increasing the output of a standardized message. The Koch Brothers, billionaires in the US known for their promotion of libertarian ideas, are said to take just such a mass-production approach to their ideological transformation work.[491] They have used this approach to great effect. Indeed, as I mentioned in the chapter on social media, the humanists also used mass production to great effect when they first got hold of the printing press in order to disseminate classical works important to their cause.

Constantly Surveying the Field

Of course, you do want to keep track of whether the individuals and organizations you are targeting are taking up the linguistic innovations you propose in the ways expected. Furthermore, you want to keep track of changes to the dominant moral language since this may affect what innovations are possible, likely, and desirable.

For example, recently those protesting COVID-19 measures have borrowed slogans from the abortion movement such as "my body, my choice" to protest laws requiring individuals to wear a mask.[492] This is a perfect example of repurposing of existing moral language so that it sparks a debate over the contours of that language (in this case a familiar debate over the line between public and private). Organizations that depend on those ideas to legitimize their work certainly have an interest in speaking out if they believe it will undermine or help their efforts.

Skinner's Theory of Change

We saw in the conventional wisdom how your goals and objectives,

---

[491] Ben Jervey, "How the Koch Network's 'Social Change' Strategy Is Built to Kill the Electric Car," *DeSmog Blog*, September 18, 2019.

[492] Marcie Bianco, "COVID-19 Mask Mandates in Wisconsin and Elsewhere Spark 'My Body My Choice' Hypocrisy," *NBC News*, Aug 3, 2020.

as well as the structure of your evaluation should track your theory of change. A theory of change can be mapped by capturing your activities, short-term outcomes, intermediate outcomes, and ultimate purpose.

The 100-Year PR Plan is predicated on Skinner's theory of how innovating ideologists have influenced political struggles in history. Understanding that theory of change will tell you what you can and should evaluate to gauge your progress. Let us therefore map Skinner's theory of change starting with the ultimate outcome, then working forward from activities.

Ultimate Outcome: A Newly Configured Moral Language

Even in undemocratic states, institutions, and social groups, decision-makers need to justify their actions to maintain legitimacy among the people they depend on to remain in power and avoid as much resistance as possible so as to avoid the cost of overcoming that resistance forcefully. Decision-makers (and their supporters) do this by describing their actions in the best way the current moral language allows.

Those interested in frustrating actions of decision-makers therefore seek to describe those actions in the most negative light the current moral language allows. Those interested in the decision-makers acting differently seek to describe the actions they desire in the best light possible so the decision-maker will be incentivized to benefit from that promised legitimacy.

The problem you as an innovator need to overcome is that existing moral languages are inadequate for the purpose of legitimizing the action you seek. The existing language may praise what you want to condemn or condemn what you want to praise. Maybe it praises what you want to praise but prioritizes something else so highly no one will ever act on your proposal. Maybe there is no word to describe what you want to praise or condemn. I have called all these problems "the justification gap".

The change the innovating ideologist wants to bring about in the world is to reconfigure the dominant moral language, so it grants and denies legitimacy so as to enable or frustrate, to the greatest extent possible, those actions the ideologist wants accomplished or stopped.[493] Changing the language therefore is a way to create the means by which to rally people and institutions to aid or oppose an action. In short, you are trying to get moral language X to get from configuration A to B.

Activities: Identifying and Propagating Linguistic Innovations

The first step is for you, the innovating ideologist, to identify as precisely as possible the limitations of configuration A as well as its inner contradictions and ambiguities. You use the terms within the dominant moral language (occasionally coining new terms) in novel ways to shift it to configuration B. Ultimately, you are trying to make your innovative use of the old language normal among decision-makers and those who influence them.

In order to do this, you often need to propose a linguistic innova-tion. In Skinner's studies, innovating ideologists do all this through works of philosophy, advice books, courses, paintings, and more. You can do it through countless mediums.

Skinner identifies some criteria that will make it more likely a linguistic innovation succeeds. It should be based on existing ways of thinking and therefore be more likely to enjoy the support of other individuals and organizations who are working on other problems but share that way of thinking. The linguistic innovation should be useful to them and help them with their struggles so that they use it often.

Short-Term Outcome: Allies Start to Use Innovation

The more the innovation is used by those who share your way of thinking, the greater the strength of the innovation will be. These allies, however, are only your most accessible targets to help provide an institutional home and some long-term structure for your innovation.

Intermediate Outcome: Getting Inside the Silent Opposition

There is a system of institutions and individuals that serve as the base to reinforce the dominant moral language. The innovating ideologist will pay special attention to these long-term institutions that maintain configuration A, such as universities, think tanks, professional associ-ations, social media networks, and others.

---

[493] Skinner, *Visions of Politics*, 149.

The innovating ideologist will try to encourage use of the linguistic innovation by those within the structure maintaining configuration A. Although the structures will naturally be resistant, by exploiting the inner contradictions and ambiguities of the dominant language, the innovating ideologist should be able to marshal support from within the dominant structures themselves. This process can take decades and is likely to be filled with conflict.

Towards the Ultimate Purpose: Seizing the Crisis

Skinner does not explicitly assign the importance to crises that I have. It may be the case that you can simply continue to incrementally build support within the existing structures, until your ideas are dominant. Nevertheless, I think I can at least say that crises offer a moment in which long-term transformations can crystallize.

Sooner or later, the decision-maker may be forced to make a choice in which they cannot maintain their legitimacy without choosing between configuration A or B. I have called this a crisis of legitimacy. They will have to choose between configuration A or B.

If the innovating ideologist has built sufficient support in the world and among those who influence the decision-maker, has chosen the right moment to force the question, and has forced the question in a sympathetic and sustainable way, then the decision-maker will be far more likely to resolve the crisis in favour of configuration B. The innovating ideologist must then maintain the pressure on the decision-maker so that configuration B is cemented as the dominant moral language.

While I have called this a theory of change, I should not be mistaken for treating this as a causal theory in the sense that if you do this it will then lead to the change you are seeking in the world (i.e., decision-maker adopts configuration B and therefore acts as you want). Skinner has written a fair bit about how ideological change can be an important factor in societal change without us necessarily needing to call it a "cause" in the scientific sense.[494] Nevertheless, it does play a causal role in the sense that it helps facilitate or prevent certain types of action. This is why the 100-Year PR Plan is always

---

[494] Skinner, *Meaning & Context*, 97-118.

incomplete and must be accompanied by other actions to actually bring about or stop the desired action.

The Gulf Between Goals and Objectives

The advice canvassed above never seems to countenance the possibility that something fundamental will be lost in shifting one's perspective from goals to objectives. If you set a truly transformative goal at the end of Chapter 3, then I would argue that there will almost certainly be an insurmountable gap between your SMART objectives and that goal.

SMART objectives are effective as motivators because they are theoretically within your power to achieve. If you set goals that are not SMART you risk complete and perpetual failure. This is highly embarrassing for you in your interactions with donors, funders, the public, those you serve, and even those within your own organization. It is also highly demoralizing for you.

The trouble is that systemic transformation is not within your power to achieve, and not just because you got the methods wrong and you should adjust. You may do everything right and still profoundly and completely fail. Systemic transformation depends on innumerable factors you do not have control over as an individual actor. Most importantly, systemic change depends on other people.

More speculatively, it may even depend on factors that humanity has little or no control over. According to Machiavelli, one of Skinner's great objects of study, fortune (all that is outside of human control) is crucial to political success, and the special skill of the politician is responding to and taking advantage of the opportunities that fortune provides.[495] We already looked at examples of this in the chapter on crisis.

This may sound demotivating. My point is that by assuming that systemic transformation can be reduced to a series of SMART objectives one risks limiting one's vision of systemic transformation to whatever can be articulated in SMART objectives.

I should not be misunderstood to be saying that you should not set SMART goals. There are things within your control. It is certainly possible for you to set useful objectives that are attainable, realistic,

---

[495] Niccolo Machiavelli (ed. & tr. David Wootton), *The Prince* (Indianapolis/Cambridge: Hackett Publishing Co., 1994), 74-76.

and timely. It is still up to you to do everything that is within your power and be held accountable accordingly.

My point is rather that if you limit your evaluation to SMART objectives, you may capture whether you have acted effectively but do not be surprised, if after all that, there is still a gulf between you and your goal. In Skinner's theory of change, you may "progress" towards your goal, and yet it may not come about for another 100 years, because some other catalyst or factor totally out of your control triggered precisely the right crisis.

Again, I acknowledge this may be a hard pill to swallow. You could work all your life to achieve a goal and it never comes. How are you supposed to motivate yourself or those who support you or work with you?

If you'll allow me to speak personally for a moment. Remember Honi at the beginning of the book who encountered the old man planting the carob tree? There is another saying worth remembering "You are not required to complete the task, yet you are not free from withdrawing from it."[496] It may well be that there is an unimaginable gulf between all that you can do and the way the world ought to be, and yet, if it is true that the world ought to be that way, then you must see your work as justified by that moral necessity and not any particular outcome.

Obviously, accepting that point of view runs contrary to the contemporary emphasis on results, for which there is much to be said. Again, I should not be taken for excusing waste or ineffectiveness. Rather, if we only do what we know to be attainable, I suspect many of the fundamental things will be left undone.

THE SOLUTION: EVALUATING YOUR 100-YEAR PR PLAN

So, given everything I said above, you may be wondering what evaluation is actually possible within the 100-Year PR Plan.

Articulating Your Theory of Change

Firstly, building on all the work you have done throughout this book you should articulate your particular theory of change:

---

[496] Ethics of Our Fathers 2: 21.

1. **Ultimate Outcome: Reconfigured Moral Language**: The configuration of the dominant moral language needed for the justification that you articulated in the exercises of Chapters 3 and 4 to mobilize a sufficient coalition of stakeholders to push the decision-maker to act.

2. **Activities: Propagation Through Justification and Use of Innovation**: You should articulate the linguistic innovation you see as necessary to get you from configuration A to B. You should list the activities you will do to propagate this innovation, being careful to separate those long-format high quality activities to justify the innovation, versus those activities in which you merely use the innovation. See exercises in chapters 6 and 8.

3. **Short-Term Outcomes: Building a Diverse Coalition of Allies**: List the potential ideological allies you identified as those you will approach with the innovation. See exercise in Chapter 7.

4. **Intermediate Outcomes: Building Support Within the Silent Opposition**: Identify the structure of the silent opposition. Your activities should aim at progressively building support within this structure for your innovation.

5. **Culminating Crisis of Legitimacy**: Here is where you articulate your crisis communications strategy that you set out in the exercise of Chapter 9.

What are You Evaluating?

In the theory of change you have just identified, there is a role for prospective, process, impact, and outcome evaluation.

Prospective Evaluation: Checking in with Allies

Firstly, I have placed a lot of stress on proposing an innovation that is based in existing ways of thinking and is useful to others who share that way of thinking, but who are facing different problems. You can evaluate the effectiveness of the linguistic innovations by reaching out to individuals at the organizations you identified as potential allies in Chapter 7 and asking them what they think. If you have the resources, you can convene a focus group to test out the innovation. To support these conversations, consider creating mock-ups of communications products in which the linguistic innovation could be used by them.

It is also useful to do traditional prospective evaluation activities to see how your audience is likely to react to your communication products. But if you have limited resources, focusing on your ideological allies is more important because they will build the institutional structure that will sustain your innovation over the long-term.

Process Evaluation: Ensuring Consistency in Language

Earlier in this chapter, I spoke about how evaluation measuring the efficiency of your process only works for transformation strategies based on quantity of output. There is, however, another sense in which process evaluation is uniquely important for ideological transformation work, and that is in the consistency of your message.

In order to spread a linguistic innovation, it is vital that your staff, volunteers, allies, or others understand the innovation and use it consistently. Auditing all your communications content in order to evaluate how your organization is using keywords is a great way to ensure everyone is pulling in the same direction.

With that being said, you should not be overly controlling, especially of allies. The point is that they will adapt your innovation to the purpose of their context. If they do this, it is often a good thing and shows the innovation has taken on a life of its own. However, if inconsistency is due to poor understanding or lack of discipline, then it will certainly limit the effectiveness of your message and make it easier to co-opt by those who want to water down its meaning.

You can evaluate the consistency of use by doing a content analysis of your own communications products. You can also conduct interviews with staff and volunteers to gauge their level of understanding of the innovation. The style guide you developed in the exercise of Chapter 6 should be integrated in all your training and on-boarding processes.

Impact Evaluation: Is Your Audience Using Your Tools

In Chapter 2 you drew a map of the existing moral language. Above I called that configuration A. Configuration A is your baseline. Every year or two, go through the same process of redrawing the map of the moral language you are interested in. Has it changed closer to configuration B? Has it changed in other ways that should change your strategy? This will give you a big picture sense of progress, but don't be surprised if you don't see any significant change for many years.

To spot more micro changes, do the exercise in Chapter 2 but with a focus on your key audiences: potential allies, but especially those within the silent opposition. Have they used your innovation at all? Have there been any new disagreements you should be following? Ultimately, the intermediate change in behaviour that you want to elicit in your audience is to use keywords in the innovative way you are proposing.

Notice that this evaluation will not necessarily tell you what your contribution to this process was. That is OK, because the function of this evaluation is learning about how to adapt your work, rather than proving its value. It is more important that you understand how things are developing that that you be able to precisely identify your contribution to it.

Outcome Evaluation: Mapping the Tectonic Shifts

If your campaign has reached a point where decision-makers have started to use an innovation you proposed or are invested in, then you can assess the outcome in the following ways.

If the innovation was to delegitimize a certain behaviour, then you will know if you were successful if the decision-maker (or their critics) use the innovation in explaining why they will or should not do something. For example, when a government makes a previously criminal act legal, they recognize that the prosecution of individuals for that act is no longer legitimate for one reason or another.

Similarly, you will know that you have succeeded to the extent that the linguistic innovation is capable of incurring consequences for the one who undertakes the challenged action. For example, when a politician resigns due to allegations of sexual harassment, this demonstrates that the labelling of certain behaviours as harassment has succeeded to the extent that it is capable of incurring consequences for even the alleged perpetrator.

If the innovation was to legitimate a certain behaviour, then similarly you will know that you have succeeded to the extent that decision-makers undertake or allow that behaviour.

For example, a company may claim it is anti-racist, environmentally friendly, or inclusive. The question is then what practical measures has the company taken on in order to back-up its claim. If it has to take on what you think those words should mean in order for it to gain the support it expects and not instead face a backlash, then you have succeeded. If it has to take on things that are different from what you intended but are nonetheless substantial, it is a sign that an innovation has cemented but its meaning is different from what you may have intended.

However, if the term is used without the consequences described above, then the term has most likely been hollowed out or co-opted. Think about the buzzwords you know. Buzzwords are where linguistic innovations go to die if they ever had substance in the first place. In some respects, buzzword status is much worse than obscurity. In obscurity, you can always claim that you are carrying the torch until the right moment to light a larger fire. However, if the word has caught on but is meaningless, then the current structures have likely effectively undermined your efforts, at least for now.

If you want to track outcomes systematically, you should record:

- A sample of incidents in which a decision-maker (or those who influence them) use your linguistic innovation
- Whether the use of the innovation seems to correspond to the innovation you intended
- The action at issue (i.e., that is either legitimized or delegitimized).
- For delegitimizing innovations:
  - whether it stopped the action or
  - what costs the application of the label to the action incurred for the actor
- For legitimizing innovations:
  - whether it promoted the intended action and
  - what costs the actor was willing to incur in order to gain the legitimacy of having the label applied to them.

Ideological Innovation Evaluation Sheet

Incident/ Source	Decision-maker	Innovative use of word	Correspondence to your proposed innovation	Did it successfully stop/enable the action?	What costs did the speaker incur to be able to use the word? What conse-quences did the use of the word have for the one being labelled?
Details of event. Source where word was used.	Name of organization or individual, position, and other relevant details.	Sense: Reference: Judgment value:	Sense: Reference: Judgment Value:	Y/N	

Chapter 11

On Living History

"...we have inherited a theory which we continue to apply, but which we do not really understand." [497]

—Quentin Skinner

In closing, it is worth reflecting on how Skinner himself sees the value of his approach to history for the wider world. In the essay from which the above quote is taken, Skinner reflects on how his method allows us to go back to a time when the ideas we now take for granted were a hotly debated choice. In seeing our ideas at those moments, we can more clearly see what purposes they were supposed to serve. This will allow us to engage our world more self-consciously, being more aware of the choices we are making, and, indeed, that they are choices at all. Through this process, we find in the past a repository of values we no longer endorse and questions we no longer ask.[498] In short, history comes to free us from the domination of the ideas of the present moment.[499]

---

[497] Skinner, *Liberty Before Liberalism*, 109-110.
[498] Skinner, *Liberty Before Liberalism*, 112.
[499] Skinner, *Liberty Before Liberalism*, 117.

It seems to me that the perspective Skinner provides comes with a moral imperative. As we become more aware of our individual and collective agency in every assumption we make and word we use, we become responsible for that agency. More than that, though, in telling stories about how people have made choices in the past, I believe Skinner has also provided us with a guide about *how* to more proactively make choices today. In fact, these two things are deeply entwined.

Every day, nonprofits face the enormity of humanity's immediate needs. This caring labour is vital for the maintenance of the world and it should never be minimized. Indeed, often those who work for nonprofits are fighting for their own survival alongside those they serve. This is especially true now as the economic crisis precipitated by COVID-19 has struck many of the sector's sources of funds precisely as demand has spiked.

Viewed from this perspective, thinking historically may seem like a luxury. In these moments, history may seem to be a privilege of the few who are comfortable enough to contemplate and who therefore speak from that comfort. History comes to be viewed in opposition to the immediate moment.

There is some practical truth in this, but history is no less a necessity for it. The trick, I think, is to not just study history but *live* historically. By "live historically" I mean two things. Firstly, in our everyday labour to maintain our world, we are conscious of how the particular forms of life we sustain are often contingent products of particular struggles we may still be engaged in. We need to be aware of where our work comes from and how it has come to take the shape it has.

This is a challenge for everyone from the newly minted volunteer to the experienced sector professional. There are so many technical skills nonprofit professionals are expected to have today that it can be easy for history of the community, of the institution, movement, or people they serve to take a back seat. If nothing else, I hope this book has inspired you to look deeper into your own work's history, and hopefully provided you with some tools to make sense of what it means for you today.

Secondly, living historically means not seeing the future as some other organization's mandate. In every act and every word, we tell the story of the world again, and this is as true on the front lines as it is elsewhere. It is not unusual to be reminded that every employee and volunteer is an informal ambassador and fundraiser. It is less common to hear that they are also authors of the unwritten constitution that is our collective moral language.

Now, it is true that some organizations do have a specific mandate to engage in policy or systems change. It makes sense that they would have more resources and time to focus on these questions. But I hope this book has reaffirmed a long-recognized lesson that no organization is an island. It is perhaps trite now to observe that everything can change overnight. But this is not just a fact to be feared and prepared for. In realizing that this change is possible, we should feel both freer and more responsible to plant and cultivate that future.

Bibliography

Abad-Santos, Alex. "How hair became a culture war in quarantine," *Vox*, June 10, 2020.https://www.vox.com/the-goods/2020/6/10/21285542/hair-cut-protest-lockdown-culture-war.

Adams, M. "From compulsory to voluntary long-form census: What we stand to lose," Ottawa: Policy Options, 2010. http://policyoptions.irpp.org/fr/magazines/afghanistan/from-compulsory-to-voluntary-long-form-census-what-we-stand-to-lose/.

Adams, Robert. *Empowerment, participation and social work*. New York: Palgrave Macmillan, 2008.

Anderson, Meghan Keaney. "How Nonprofits Can Use Measurement To Adapt to the Facebook Algorithm Change," Beth's Blog, October 16, 2012. http://www.bethkanter.org/facebook-tactics/.

Akerley, Courtney. "What Will Be the Long-Term Impact of the #MeToo Movement?" University of Connecticut, November 5, 2018. https://www.business.uconn.edu/2018/11/05/what-will-be-the-long-term-impact-of-the-metoo-movement/.

Aizenman, Nurith. "How To Demand A Medical Breakthrough: Lessons From The AIDS Fight," *National Public Radio*, February 9, 2019. https://www.npr.org/sections/health-shots/2019/02/09/689924838/how-to-demand-a-medical-breakthrough-lessons-from-the-aids-fight.

Alexandra, Kayleigh. "5 Examples Of Nonprofit Social Media Strategies (And What You Can Learn From Them)," *Wild Apricot*, November 7, 2019. https://www.wildapricot.com/blogs/newsblog/2019/11/07/nonprofit-social-media-strategy.

Ashton, Amanda. "Competitive Analysis: Why Your Nonprofit Needs to Size-Up the Competition," Change Better, December 3, 2018. https://medium.com/changebetter/competitive-analysis-why-your-nonprofit-needs-to-size-up-the-competition-2c4323f1ba91.

Aust, Anthony. *Handbook of International Law* (2nd ed.). Cambridge: Cambridge University Press, 2010.

Azelrad, Claire. "The 9 Signs of a Successful Social Media Strategy for Nonprofits," NealSchaffer.com, 2017. https://nealschaffer.com/social-media-strategy-for-nonprofits/.

Barman, E. A. "Asserting difference: The strategic response of nonprofit organizations to competition," *Social Forces* 80 no.4 (2002): 1191-1222. doi:http://dx.doi.org.myaccess.library.utoronto.ca/10.1353/sof.2002.0020.

Michel Bauwens, Alex Pazaitis, P2P Accounting for Planetary Survival. P2P Foundation, 2019 https://p2pfoundation.net/wp-content/uploads/2019/06/AccountingForPlanetarySurvival_def.pdf.

Beckett-Maines, Melinda. "Strategies to Up Your Crisis Management Game," *Nonprofit Communications Report* 17 no. 2 (February 2019): 7.

Bianco, Marcie. "COVID-19 Mask Mandates in Wisconsin and Elsewhere Spark 'My Body My Choice' Hypocrisy," *NBC News*, Aug 3, 2020. https://www.nbcnews.com/think/opinion/covid-19-mask-mandates-wisconsin-elsewhere-spark-my-body-my-ncna1235535.

Bogost, Ian. "The Rhetoric of Video Games," *The Ecology of Games: Connecting Youth, Games, and Learning*. Ed. by Katie Salen. The John D. and Catherine T. MacArthur Foundation Series on Digital Media and Learning. Cambridge, MA: The MIT Press, 2016.

Bonk, Kathy, Henry Griggs, Phil Sparks, and Emily Tynes. *Strategic Communications for Nonprofits: A Step-by-Step Guide to Working with the Media*. San Francisco: Jossey-Bass, A Wiley Imprint, 2008.

Brinckerhoff, Peter C. *Mission-based marketing: positioning your not-for-profit in an increasingly competitive world*. Hoboken, New Jersey: John Wiley & Sons, 2010.

Brock, Dan. "Ethical Issues in the Use of Cost Effectiveness Analysis for the Prioritization of Health Resources," In *Handbook of Bioethics*, vol 78, edited by G. Khushf. Dordrecht: Kluwer, 2004. https://doi.org/10.1007/1-4020-2127-5_1.

Burman, Dilshad. "Toronto's safe injection sites: your FAQs answered," Aug 14, 2018, *CityTV News*, https://toronto.citynews.ca/2018/08/14/toronto-safe-injection-site-faq/.

CallHub. "4 Steps For An Effective Nonprofit Communications Strategy," CallHub, 2020. https://callhub.io/nonprofit-communications-strategy/.

Campbell, Julia. "Steps to a Successful Nonprofit Social Media Strategy," *The Balance SMB*, July 16, 2019. https://www.thebalancesmb.com/nonprofit-social-media-steps-2502531.

Carter, Adam. "Military report reveals what sector has long known: Ontario's nursing homes are in trouble," *CBC Toronto*, May 27, 2020. https://www.cbc.ca/news/canada/toronto/military-long-term-care-home-report-covid-ontario-1.5585844.

Carboni, Julia and Sarah Maxwell. "Effective Social Media Engagement for Nonprofits: What Matters?" *Journal of Public and Nonprofit Affairs*, 2015. https://www.researchgate.net/publication/294425714_Effective_Social_Media_Engagement_for_Nonprofits_What_Matters.

Clark, Campbell. "Trudeau Betting Most Canadians Don't Care About Deficits," *The Globe and Mail*, March 24, 2016. https://www.theglobeandmail.com/news/politics/globe-politics-insider/trudeaus-liberals-seem-to-be-undoing-years-of-political-conditioning-against-deficits/article29375009/.

Chapman, David, Katrina Miller-Stevens, John C. Morris and Brendan O'Hallarn. "Social Media as a Tool for Nonprofit Advocacy and Civic Engagement: A Case Study of Blue Star Families," *Social Media and Networking*, (Hershey, PA., IGI Global), 66 – 93.

Asencio, Hugo and Sun, Rui, ed., *Cases on Strategic Social Media Utilization in the Nonprofit Sector*, edited by Hugo Asencio and Rui Sun (Information Science Reference, 2015), 66-93.

Cheung, I. W. "Plain language to minimize cognitive load: A social justice perspective," *IEEE Transactions on Professional Communication* 60, no. 4 (2017): 448-457. DOI: 10.1109/TPC.2017.2759639.

Chia, Joy L. "'What's Love Got to Do with It?': LGBTQ Rights and Patriotism in Xi's China," *Australian Journal of Asian Law* 20, no. 1 (2019). SSRN: https://ssrn.com/abstract=3491038.

Chicago Tribune, "#MeToo: A timeline of events," Chicago Tribune, 2017-2020. https://www.chicagotribune.com/lifestyles/ct-me-too-timeline-20171208-htmlstory.html.

Cody, Janay. "Why PhDs Shouldn't Overlook A Career with A Nonprofit Organization," *Cheeky Scientist* (2020). https://cheekyscientist.com/why-phds-shouldnt-overlook-a-career-with-a-nonprofit-organization/.

Comunello, F., S. Mulargia, and L. Parisi. "The 'Proper' Way to Spread Ideas through Social Media: Exploring the Affordances and Constraints of Different Social Media Platforms as Perceived by Italian Activists," *The Sociological Review* 64 no.3 (2016) 515–532.https://doi.org/10.1111/1467-954X.12378.

Condren, Melinda, and Claire McWatt. "From the Bottom Up: A Growth Strategy for Grassroots Groups in Ontario," Grassroots Growth/Volunteer Toronto, 2017. https://cdn.ymaws.com/www.volunteertoronto.ca/resource/resmgr/Files/From_The_Bottom_Up_Report_-_.pdf.

Conrardy, Alyssa. "Build a Better Nonprofit Marketing Plan: Here's How." *Prosper Strategies*, 2018. https://prosper-strategies.com/inspiring-nonprofit-marketing-plan-example/.

Creal, Spencer. "Why Competition in the Nonprofit Sector is Frustrating," Nonprofit Hub, November 15, 2017. https://nonprofithub.org/starting-a-nonprofit/strange-and-frustrating-competition-of-nonprofit-sector/.

CTV.ca News Staff. "Manitoba, Ontario among provinces backing long census," *CTV News*, July 20, 2010. http://www.ctvnews.ca/manitoba-ontario-among-provinces-backing-long-census-1.534318.

Dan, Michael, David B. MacDonald, and Bernie M. Farber. "Should Statues of John A MacDonald be removed?" *Toronto Star*, August 21, 2018. https://www.thestar.com/opinion/contributors/thebigdebate/2018/08/21/should-statues-of-sir-john-a-macdonald-be-removed-yes.html.

Davenport, Deborah. "Strategic Communication Impact in the nonprofit sector," Brian Lamb School of Communications, Purdue University. https://cla.purdue.edu/academic/communication/graduate/online/strategic-communications-for-non-profit-organizations.html.

Dehaas, Josh. "Election Analysis: Most Common Occupation for Candidates in Each Party," *CTV News*, October 9, 2015. https://www.ctvnews.ca/politics/election/election-analysis-most-common-occupations-for-candidates-in-each-party-1.2602533.

Dewitt, Brydon M. *The Nonprofit Development Companion: A workbook for fundraising success.* Hoboken, New Jersey: John Wiley & Sons, Inc., 2011.

Dolnicar, Sara; Leisch, Friedrich and Randle, Melanie. "Competition or collaboration? The effect of non-profit brand image on volunteer recruitment strategy," *Journal of Brand Management* 20 no.8 (September 2013): 689-704. doi:http://dx.doi.org.myaccess.library.utoronto.ca/10.1057/bm.2013.9.

Draves, Bill. *The Free University: A Model for Lifelong Learning.* Chicago, Illinois: Association Press, Follett Publishing Company, 1980.

Drummond, Michael. "Allocating Resources," *International Journal of Technology Assessment in Health Care*, Volume 6, Issue 1 (January 1990, pp. 77-92).

Eakin, Lynn. "We can't afford to do business this way," Wellesley Institute, 2007. http://lynneakin.com/frameset//images/LE_Docs/Reports/FinancingtheNonprofitSector/WeCantAffordtoDoBusinessThisWay/we-cant-afford-to-do-business-this-way-colour.pdf.

Ell, Diane. "Evaluation of Communications," SaskCulture, 2020. https://www.saskculture.ca/programs/organizational-support/organizational-resources?resource=11&subresource=69.

English, Dayton. "Strategic Communication Objectives for Nonprofit Organizations", Chron. https://smallbusiness.chron.com/strategic-communication-objectives-nonprofit-organizations-64903.html.

Fellegi, I. "Statistics, public confidence and lessons from the story of the 2011 Canadian Census [PPT]." Presented in Manotick at slide 4. August 1, 2012. http://www.probusorv.org/presentations/2012-08-01-Fellegi.pdf.

Ferguson, Sian. "Calling In: A Quick Guide on When and How," *Everyday Feminist*, January 17, 2015. https://everydayfeminism.com/2015/01/guide-to-calling-in/.

Folkman, Joseph. "The 6 Key Secrets to Increasing Empowerment in Your Team," *Forbes*, March 2, 2017. https://www.forbes.com/sites/joefolkman/2017/03/02/the-6-key-secrets-to-increasing-empowerment-in-your-team/#71f254277a65.

Forsey, Eugene A. "King-Byng Affair," *The Canadian Encyclopedia*, March 4, 2015. https://www.thecanadianencyclopedia.ca/en/article/king-byng-affair.

Frumkin, Peter. *On Being Nonprofit: A Conceptual and Policy Primer.* Cambridge, Massachusetts: Harvard University Press, 2005.

Frumkin, Peter, and Suzi Sosa. "Competitive Positioning: Why Knowing Your Competition Is Essential to Social Impact Success," *Non-Profit Quarterly*, March 20, 2018. https://nonprofitquarterly.org/competitive-positioning-why-knowing-your-competition-is-essential-to-social-impact-success/.

Fulton, Otis, and Katrina VanHuss. "Sizing Up Your Nonprofit Competition," *NonprofitPro*, April 18, 2018. https://www.nonprofitpro.com/post/sizing-nonprofit-competition/.

Gamble, Ione. "In defence of tumblr feminism," *Dazed*, April 8, 2016. https://www.dazeddigital.com/artsandculture/article/30679/1/in-defence-of-tumblr-feminism.

Geller, Corinne. "Four Tips for Navigating a Crisis," *Nonprofit Communications Report* 17 no. 1 (December 10, 2018): 4.

Greenwald, Michelle. "What's Really Driving The Limitless Growth Of Podcasts," *Forbes*, October 4, 2018. https://www.forbes.com/sites/michellegreenwald/2018/10/04/why-podcasts-will-continue-to-grow-why-its-great-for-brands/#78c4f739205f.

Gilbert, David. "Here's How Big Far Right Social Network Gab Has Actually Gotten," *Vice*, August 16, 2019. https://www.vice.com/en_ca/article/pa7dwg/heres-how-big-far-right-social-network-gab-has-actually-gotten.

Haas, J. *The assassination of Fred Hampton: How the FBI and the Chicago police murdered a Black Panther.* Chicago, Illinois: Lawrence Hill Books/Chicago Review Press, 2010.

Hager, Mark and Elizabeth Searing. "10 Ways to Kill Your Nonprofit," *Nonprofit Quarterly*, (Winter 2014), January 6, 2015. https://nonprofitquarterly.org/10-ways-to-kill-your-nonprofit/.

Hart, James D. and Phillip Leininger. *The Oxford Companion to American Literature.* Oxford: Oxford University Press, 1995. ISBN 9780195065480.

Hebert, Camille L. "Is MeToo Only a Social Movement or a Legal Movement Too?" *Emp. Rts. & Emp. Pol'y J.* 22 (2018) 321.

Henley, Terri Kline, Donald Self, and Walter W. Wymer, Jr. *Marketing Communications for Local Nonprofit Organizations: Targets and Tools.* New York: Routledge, 2011.

Hiebert, Paul. "Here's Why Ads That Celebrate Eating in Secret Work," *AdWeek*, December 2, 2019. https://www.adweek.com/brand-marketing/heres-why-ads-that-celebrate-eating-in-secret-work/.

Ihm, Jennifer. "Communicating without nonprofit organizations on nonprofits' social media: Stakeholders' autonomous networks and three types of organizational ties," *New Media & Society* 21 no.11-12 (2019): 2648–2670. https://doi.org/10.1177/1461444819854806.

INCITE! (Ed.) *The Revolution Will Not Be Funded: Beyond the Non-Profit Industrial Complex.* Durham; London: Duke University Press, 2007. doi:10.2307/j.ctv11smnz6.

Jervey, Ben. "How the Koch Network's 'Social Change' Strategy Is Built to Kill the Electric Car," *DeSmog Blog*, September 18, 2019. https://www.desmogblog.com/2019/09/19/koch-network-structure-social-change-kill-electric-car.

Kania, John and Mark Kramer. "Collective Impact," *Stanford Social Innovation Review*, Winter 2011. https://ssir.org/articles/entry/collective_impact.

Kanter, Beth. "Can Memes for Good Work for your Nonprofit's Content Strategy? Not on Facebook!" Beth's Blog, September 6, 2013. http://www.bethkanter.org/memes-good/.

Kavner, Lucas. "At Brooklyn Free School, A Movement Reborn with Liberty And No Testing For All," *The Huffington Post*, November 30, 2012. https://www.huffingtonpost.ca/entry/brooklyn-free-school-_n_2214263?ri18n=true.

Keegan, Lewis. "79+ Staggering Online Learning Statistics! (All You Need to Know!)" *Skillscouter*, May 7 2020. Available at: https://skillscouter.com/online-learning-statistics/.

Kilcullen, David. "Land of the fearful, home of the heavily armed and hateful," *The Australian*, May 30, 2020. https://www.theaustralian.com.au/inquirer/land-of-the-fearful-home-of-the-heavily-armed-and-hateful/news-story/6ec95cf2dd7ea519d084ed99dc3fd450.

Kinzey, Ruth Ellen. *Promoting nonprofit organizations: a reputation management approach.* New York: Routledge, 2013.

Kyff, Rob. "20 most important Neologisms of Century," *The Hartford Courant*, December 8, 1999. https://www.courant.com/news/connecticut/hc-xpm-1999-12-08-9912081606-story.html.

Lampe, Clifford, Jonathan A. Obar, and Paul Zube. "Advocacy 2.0: An Analysis of How Advocacy Groups in the United States Perceive and Use Social Media as Tools for Facilitating Civic Engagement and Collective Action," *Journal of Information Policy* 2, (2012): 1-25. https://www.jstor.org/stable/10.5325/jinfopoli.2.2012.0001.

Lee, Allan, Amy Wei Tian, and Sara Willis. "When Empowering Employees Works, and When It Doesn't," *Harvard Business Review*, March 2, 2018. https://hbr.org/2018/03/when-empowering-employees-works-and-when-it-doesnt.

Lee, Kevan. "Social Media for Non-Profits: High-Impact Tips and the Best Free Tools," *Buffer*. https://buffer.com/library/social-media-non-profits/.

Levy, Roee, and Martin Mattsson. "The Effects of Social Movements: Evidence from #MeToo," Yale University, March 30, 2020. https://papers.ssrn.com/sol3/papers.cfm?abstract_id=3496903.

Lile, Samantha. "17 Creative Visual Marketing Campaigns by Nonprofits," *The Complete Guide to Nonprofit Marketing*, 2017. https://visme.co/blog/nonprofit-marketing/.

Lysakowski, Linda. *Nonprofit Essentials: The Development Plan.* Hoboken, New Jersey: John Wiley & Sons, Inc., 2007.

Machiavelli, Niccolo. *The Discourses.* New York: Penguin Books, 2003.

Machiavelli, Niccolo. "The Prince, Chapter 25: How much fortune can achieve in human affairs and how it is to be resisted," In Selected Political Writings (ed. & tr. David Wootton). Indianapolis/Cambridge: Hackett Publishing Company, 1994 (1512).

Mackey, Peter. "The 'Five P's' of Strategic Nonprofit Storytelling," *Storytelling Procedures*, Feb 12, 2018.

Malesh, Patricia M., Sharon McKenzie Stevens. *Active Voices: Composing a Rhetoric for Social Movements*. New York: State University of New York, 2009.

Mayer, Jane. *Dark Money: The Secret History of the Billionaires Behind the Rise of the Radical Right*. New York: Anchor Books, 2017.

McIlroy-Young, Reid, and Ashton Anderson. "From 'Welcome New Gabbers' to the Pittsburgh Synagogue Shooting: The Evolution of Gab," *Proceedings of the International AAAI Conference on Web and Social Media* 13, no.1 (December 24, 2019): 651-654 https://arxiv.org/abs/1912.11278.

McDaniel, S., and H. MacDonald. "To Know Ourselves—Not," *The Canadian Journal of Sociology /Cahiers Canadiens De Sociologie* 37 no.3 (2012): 253-271.

McNeil, Joanne. "From Anon to Alt-Right: The Dangerous Tricksters of 4chan On the Evolution of Online Toxicity," *Literary Hub*, March 2, 2020. https://lithub.com/from-anon-to-alt-right-the-dangerous-tricksters-of-4chan/.

Miller, Benjamin. "The Intrusion of Real Life into Philosophy: The Pedagogical, Methodological, and Political Implications of Acknowledging We Have Other Stuff Going On," *Half a Maven*, June 2, 2020. http://halfamaven.wordpress.com/2020/06/02/the-intrusion-of-real-life-into-philosophy-the-pedagogical-methodological-and-political-implications-of-acknowledging-we-have-other-stuff-going-on/.

Miller, Benjamin. "The Temptations of Modern Silence," *Half a Maven*, July 9, 2017. https://halfamaven.wordpress.com/2017/07/09/the-temptations-of-a-modern-silence/.

Miller, Benjamin. "The People and the Experts: What Each Knows and What it Means for Politics," *Half a Maven*, January 22, 2018. https://halfamaven.wordpress.com/2018/01/22/the-people-and-the-experts-what-each-knows-and-what-it-means-for-politics/.

Miller, Benjamin. "Democratic Dialogue and the Political Art of Listening," *Half a Maven*, September 18, 2019. https://halfamaven.wordpress.com/2019/09/18/democratic-dialogue-and-the-political-art-of-listening/.

Miller, Benjamin. "Striking the Right Regulatory Balance May be Key to Helping Canada Avoid the Creep of 'Dark Money' that has Infiltrated Politics and Philanthropy South of the Border," *The Philanthropist*, March 2, 2020. https://thephilanthropist.ca/2020/03/the-right-regulatory-balance-may-be-key-to-helping-canada-avoid-the-creep-of-dark-money-that-has-infiltrated-politics-and-philanthropy-south-of-the-border/.

Miller, Benjamin. "Theorizing Legal Needs: Towards a Caring Legal System." (thesis), University of Ottawa, 2016. https://ruor.uottawa.ca/bitstream/10393/35204/9/Miller_Benjamin_2016_Thesis.pdf.

Miller, Kivi Leroux. "27 Communications and Marketing Tactics for Nonprofits," *Nonprofit Marketing Guide*, 2019. https://www.nonprofitmarketingguide.com/blog/2019/01/03/27-communications-marketing-tactics-nonprofits/.

MissionBox staff, "Drafting a Nonprofit Communications Strategy," *Missionbox*, April 1, 2020. https://www.missionbox.com/article/24/drafting-a-nonprofit-communications-strategy.

Moldenhauer, Jearld Frederick. "Toronto Gay Action, The Gay Alliance Toward Equality and CHAT," *Canadian Gay Movement: History of Activism*. http://www.jearldmoldenhauer.com/toronto-gay-action-gay-alliance-toward-equality-chat/.

Morand, Tatiana. "How to Create a Crisis Communications Plan for Your Nonprofit," *Wild Apricot*, March 20, 2020. https://www.wildapricot.com/blogs/newsblog/2020/03/20/nonprofit-crisis-communications-plan.

Munro, Andre. "Quentin Skinner," *Encyclopedia Britannica*, 2019. https://www.britannica.com/biography/Quentin-Skinner.

National Empowerment Centre, "The Ex-Patients' Movement: Where We've Been and Where We're Going." *The Journal of Mind and Behavior* 11, no. 3, (Summer 1990): 323-336. https://power2u.org/the-ex-patients-movement where-weve-been-and-where-were-going/.

Nevitte, Neil. *The Decline of Deference: Canadian Value Change in Cross National Perspective.* Toronto: University of Toronto Press, 1996.

North, Anna, "7 positive changes that have come from the #MeToo movement," *Vox*, October 4, 2019. https://www.vox.com/identities/2019/10/4/20852639/me-too-movement-sexual-harassment-law-2019.

Oakeshott, Michael. *Rationalism in Politics and Other Essays.* Indianapolis: Liberty Fund, 1991.

Ohlheiser, Abby. "How #MeToo really was different according to data," *The Washington Post*, October 7, 2018. http://108.166.64.190/omeka222/files/original/be976bf88abbc8b6b6424c1c444773a1.pdf.

Ongenaert, David. "Refugee Organizations' Public Communication: Conceptualizing and Exploring New Avenues for an Underdeveloped Research Subject," *Media and Communication* 7, no. 2, 195–206. DOI:10.17645/mac.v7i2.1953.

Pallotta, Dan. "The Way We Think About Charity is Dead Wrong," TED2013 Talks, March 2013. https://www.ted.com/talks/dan_pallotta_the_way_we_think_about_charity_is_dead_wrong/transcript?language=e

Patterson, Sally J., and Radtke, Janel M. *Strategic Communications for Nonprofit Organizations: Seven Steps to Creating a Successful Plan: Second Edition.* Hoboken, New Jersey: John Wiley & Sons, 2009. doi:10.1002/9781118386804.

Payne, Ed, and Chandler Friedman. "Viral ad campaign hits #FirstWorldProblems," *CNN*, October 23, 2012. https://www.cnn.com/2012/10/23/tech/ad-campaign-twist/index.html.

Poole, Thomas. "Leviathan in Lockdown," *London Review of Books*, May 2020. https://www.lrb.co.uk/blog/2020/may/leviathan-in-lockdown.

Pough, Gwendolyn D. "Empowering Rhetoric: Black Students Writing Black Panthers," *College Composition and Communication* 53 no. 3 (Feb. 2002): 466-486.

Pride Toronto. "Pride Toronto: Economic Impact Report 2019", *Pride Toronto*, 2019. https://www.pridetoronto.com/wp-content/uploads/2019/12/Pride-Toronto_Economic-Impact-Report-2019.pdf.

Ranciere, Jacques. *The Politics of Aesthetics*. London: Bloomsbury, 2013.

Rappaport, Julian. "In praise of paradox: A social policy of empowerment over prevention," *American Journal of Community Psychology* 9 no.1 (1981): 1–25.

Raymond, Susan. *Recession, Recovery and Renewal*. John Wiley & Sons, Inc., 2013.

Rawlins, Michael D. and Anthony J. Culyer. "National Institute for Clinical Excellence and its Value Judgments," *British Medical Journal*, (2004): 329.

Room, Robin. "Alcoholics Anonymous as a Social Movement," Addiction Research Foundation, 1993. https://www.robinroom.net/alcoanon.htm.

Schmid, Alex P. *The Routledge Handbook of Terrorism Research*. New York: Routledge, 2011.

Shannon, Meg. "How to create a crisis communications plan for your nonprofit organization," Nonprofit Mar Community, December 3, 2015. https://nonprofitmarcommunity.com/crisis-communications-plan/.

Siddiqui, Haroon. "Gutting of census stirs opposition to Stephen Harper," *Toronto Star*, July 10, 2010. https://www.thestar.com/news/canada/2010/07/10/siddiqui_gutting_of_census_stirs_opposition_to_stephen_harper.html.

Skinner, Quentin. *Liberty before Liberalism*. Cambridge: Cambridge University Press, 1998.

Skinner, Quentin. "Interview Transcript." *Making History: The Changing Face of the Profession in Britain*. Interview by Anonymous Project Officer. April 18, 2008. https://archives.history.ac.uk/makinghistory/resources/interviews/Skinner_Quentin.html.

Skinner, Quentin. "'Social meaning' and the explanation of social action," in *Visions of Politics*, 128-144. Cambridge: Cambridge University Press, 2002. doi:10.1017/CBO9780511790812.010.

Skinner, Quentin. "Moral principles and social change," in *Visions of Politics*, 145-157. Cambridge: Cambridge University Press, 2002. doi:10.1017/CBO9780511790812.011.

Skinner, Quentin. "The idea of a cultural lexicon," in *Visions of Politics*, 158-174. Cambridge: Cambridge University Press, 2002. doi:10.1017/CBO9780511790812.012.

Skinner, Quentin. "Retrospect: Studying rhetoric and conceptual change," in *Visions of Politics*, 175-187. Cambridge: Cambridge University Press, 2002. doi:10.1017/CBO9780511790812.013.

Skinner, Quentin. "Meaning and Understanding in the History of Ideas," in *Meaning & Context: Quentin Skinner and his Critics*, edited by James Tully, 29-67. Princeton: Princeton University Press, 1988.

Skinner, Quentin. "Social Meaning and The Explanation of Social Action." In *Meaning & Context: Quentin Skinner and his Critics*, edited by James Tully, 79-96. Princeton: Princeton University Press, 1988.

Skinner, Quentin. *The Foundations of Modern Political Thought Volume One: The Renaissance*. Cambridge: Cambridge University Press, 1998.

Skinner, Quentin. *The Foundations of Modern Political Thought Volume Two: The Age of Reformation*. Cambridge: Cambridge University Press, 2004. doi:10.1017/CBO9780511817892.

Skinner, Quentin. "III. Some Problems in the Analysis of Political Thought and Action," *Political Theory* 2 no. 3. (August 1, 1974): 277-303. doi.org/10.1177/009059177400200303.

Skinner, Quentin. *From Humanism to Hobbes*. Cambridge: Cambridge University Press, 2018.

Skinner, Quentin. *Visions of Politics Volume 2, Renaissance Virtues*. Cambridge: Cambridge University Press, 2002.

Quentin Skinner, *Visions of Politics, Volume 3, Hobbes and Civil Science*. Cambridge: University of Cambridge, 2002.

Smarp. "Empowerment in the Workplace: Definition & Best Practices," Smarp, December 19, 2019 https://blog.smarp.com/empowerment-in-the-workplace-enable-your-employees.

Social Media Group. "GOING SOCIAL: Tapping into Social Media for Nonprofit Success," Convio Services Team, 2010. http://www.convio.com/files/Convio_Social-Media-Guide-DevR2.pdf.

Smith, T. "Changing Racial Labels: From 'Colored' to 'Negro' to 'Black' to 'African American'", *The Public Opinion Quarterly* 56 no. 4 (1992) 496-514.

Statistics Canada. "Chapter 4—Content determination" in *Guide to the Census of Population*, 2016. Government of Canada. http://www12.statcan.gc.ca/census-recensement/2016/ref/98-304/chap4-eng.cfm.

Stewart, Amanda. "Understanding nonprofit professionalization: Common concepts and new directions for research", (student paper) August 2014. https://www.sp2.upenn.edu/wp-content/uploads/2014/08/Amanda-Stewart.pdf.

Stone, Deborah A. *Policy Paradox: The Art of Political Decision-Making*. New York: W. W. Norton and Co Inc., 2012.

The Canadian Press. "One year later: A look back at how the Fort McMurray wildfires unfolded," Bloomberg, May 1, 2017. https://www.bnnbloomberg.ca/a-look-back-at-how-the-fort-mcmurray-wildfires-unfolded-1.739324.

Tully, James. "The pen is a mightier sword: Quentin Skinner's analysis of politics" In *Meaning & Context: Quentin Skinner and his Critics*, edited by James Tully, 7-28. Princeton: Princeton University Press, 1988.

Thunberg, Greta. "'Our house is on fire': Greta Thunberg, 16, urges leaders to act on climate," *The Guardian*, January 25, 2019. https://www.theguardian.com/environment/2019/jan/25/our-house-is-on-fire-greta-thunberg16-urges-leaders-to-act-on-climate.

Tsekouras, Phil. "City of Toronto votes unanimously to declare climate emergency", *CTV News*, October 2, 2019. https://toronto.ctvnews.ca/city-of-toronto-votes-unanimously-to-declare-climate-emergency-1.4620611.

Tronto, Joan. *Caring Democracy: Markets, Equality and Justice*. New York: NYU Press, 2013.

University of Toronto. "Heritage plaque honours Ontario's first gay and lesbian rights group," *U of T News*, November 3, 2011. https://www.utoronto.ca/news/heritage-plaque-honours-ontarios-first-gay-and-lesbian-rights-group.

Upright, Paula, and Kristeen Tice-Owens. "Crisis Management in Nonprofit Organizations: A Case Study of Crisis Communication and Planning," *Journal of Nonprofit Education and Leadership* 6, no. 2, (2016): 159–177.

Volpe, Allie. "It's not all Pepes and trollfaces—memes can be a force for good," *The Verge*, August 27, 2018. https://www.theverge.com/2018/8/27/17760170/memes-good-behavioral-science-nazi-pepe.

Walker, Jeffrey C. "Solving the World's Biggest Problems: Better Philanthropy Through Systems Change," *Stanford Social Innovation Review*, Apr. 5, 2017. https://ssir.org/articles/entry/better_philanthropy_through_systems_change.

Weinger, Adam. "4 Strategies to Nonprofit Social Media Marketing," NonProfitPro, Aug 28, 2018. https://www.nonprofitpro.com/post/4-strategies-to-nonprofit-social-media-marketing/.

Wiggill, Marlene. "Strategic communication management in the nonprofit sector: a simplified model," *Journal of Public Affairs* 11, no.4, (2011): 226-235.

Williams, David. *Marketing & Communications in Nonprofit Organizations: It Matters More Than You Think, Essays on Excellence.* Georgetown: Centre for Nonprofit Leadership and Georgetown University, 2009. https://www.bernuthconsulting.com/wp-content/uploads/Georgetown-CPNL-nonprofit-marketing-whitepaper.pdf.

Wonder, Stacey. "4 Easy Steps to Develop a Social Media Content Strategy for Your Nonprofit," Guidestar Blog, November 20, 2018. https://trust.guidestar.org/4-easy-steps-to-develop-a-social-media-content-strategy-for-your-nonprofit.

Wood, Molly. "More extremists are getting radicalized online. Whose responsibility is that?" *Marketplace*, March 13, 2019. https://www.marketplace.org/2019/03/19/extremists-are-being-radicalized-online-whose-responsibility-is-it/.

Wright, Amanda. "Challenges in achieving non-profit sustainability: a study of the social service non-profit sector in the central Okanagan," Scotiabank Centre for Non-Profit Excellence, 2015. https://www.okanagan.bc.ca/Assets/Departments+(Education)/Business/Documents/NPC+Survey+Report.pdf.

Yeo, M. "The Rights of Science and the Rights of Politics: Lessons from the Long-form Census Controversy," *The Canadian Journal of Sociology/Cahiers canadiens de sociologie* 37 no.3 (September 2012): 295-317.

***

"About," Me Too Movement, 2020. https://metoomvmt.org/about/.

"About Us," Education Superhighway. https://www.educationsuperhighway.org/about/.

"Advocacy," Wikipedia. https://en.wikipedia.org/wiki/Wikipedia:Advocacy.

"Be the Change You Wish to See in the World," Quote Investigator. https://quoteinvestigator.com/2017/10/23/be-change/.

"Best Nonprofit Communication Strategies," Queens University of Charlotte, 2020. https://online.queens.edu/online-programs/macomm/resources/nonprofit-communication-strategies.

"Bits and Pieces," CHAT (Community Homophile Association Of Toronto). https://www.onthebookshelves.com/chat.htm.

"Canadian Definition of Homelessness," Canadian Observatory on Homelessness. https://www.homelesshub.ca/sites/default/files/COHhomelessdefinition.pdf.

"Chauvinism," Online Etymology Dictionary. https://www.etymonline.com/word/chauvinism.

"Communicating During a Crisis," Nonprofit Risk Management Center, 2020. https://nonprofitrisk.org/resources/articles/communicating-during-a-crisis/.

"Crisis Communication Plan Nonprofit Toolkit," Colorado Nonprofit Association. https://sustainingplaces.files.wordpress.com/2014/03/crisiscomm.pdf.

"Decent Work," Ontario Nonprofit Network, https://theonn.ca/our-work/our-people/decent-work/.

"eBooks-Worldwide," Statista, 2020. https://www.statista.com/outlook/213/100/ebooks/worldwide.

"Ecological Footprint: Overview," Global Footprint Network. Footprintnetwork.org.

"Edgelord," Dictionary.com. https://www.dictionary.com/e/slang/edgelord/.

"Empowerment," Lexico, 2020. https://www.lexico.com/en/definition/empowerment.

"Five Tips for Communicating Through a Crisis," *Nonprofit Communications Report* 14 no. 8 (July 20 2016): 3.

"Guest Blogs by Sector: Non-Profit," PhDs at Work. https://phdsatwork.com/week-in-the-life/sector/non-profit/.

"Guidelines for Evaluating Nonprofit Communications Efforts," Communications Consortium Media Center, April 2004. http://www.pointk.org/resources/files/Eval_comm_efforts.pdf.

"Historical Data: the birth of AA and its Growth in the US and Canada," Alcoholics Anonymous. https://www.aa.org/pages/en_US/historical-data-the-birth-of-aa-and-its-growth-in-the-uscanada

"How to create a communications plan for your nonprofit," Tatiana Morand https://www.wildapricot.com/blogs/newsblog/2020/03/20/nonprofit-crisis-communications-plan.

"How to Define Your Target Audience: Is Your Nonprofit a Match for Your Community?" Network for Good, June 22, 2010. https://prosper-strategies.com/inspiring-nonprofit-marketing-plan-example/.

"How to Handle Crisis Communication," Shea Davis, Nonprofit Communications Report https://www.readcube.com/articles/10.1002%2Fnpcr.30614.

"It Just Got Weird," Ottawa Coalition to End Violence Against Women. http://justgotweird.com/.

"Millennials in the Nonprofit Sector," KDP Consulting. https://kdpconsulting.ca/millennials-in-a-nonprofit-sector/.

"Nazi Salute GIFS," Tenor, https://tenor.com/search/nazi-salute-GIFS.

Heather Mansfield, Nonprofit Tech for Good https://www.nptechforgood.com/heather-mansfield/.

"PETA Pokemon Black and Blue," PETA. https://games.peta.org/pokemon-black-and-white-parody/.

"Pride In Canada," The Canadian Encyclopedia, June 28, 2016. https://www.thecanadianencyclopedia.ca/en/article/world-pride-2014-toronto.

"Proud Boys," Southern Poverty Law Center, 2020. https://www.splcenter.org/fighting-hate/extremist-files/group/proud-boys.

"Show Grace Under Pressure During a Crisis," *Nonprofit Communications Report 14* no. 4 (March 15, 2016): 4.

"Social Media for Non-Profits: High-Impact Tips and the Best Free Tools," Kevan Lee, Buffer (n.d).

"Terrorism," Online Etymology Dictionary, 2020. https://www.etymonline.com/word/terrorism.

"The Communication Plan," SaskCulture, https://www.saskculture.ca/programs/organizational-support/organizational-resources?resource=11&subresource=63.

"Upleaf Nonprofit Communication Plan Template," Upleaf Technology Solutions. https://upleaf.com/nonprofit-resources/strategy-design/communication-plan-template/.

"Vegan Philosophy and Lifestyle," Vegan Society of Canada, accessed May 18, 2020. https://www.vegancanada.org/.

"What is Strategic Communications?" Idea.org, March 16, 2011, https://www.idea.org/blog/2011/03/16/what-is-strategic-communications/.

"What is the Social License?" Shinglespit Consultants, 2020, https://socialicense.com/definition.html.

www.ingramcontent.com/pod-product-compliance
Lightning Source LLC
Chambersburg PA
CBHW061158220326
41599CB00025B/4522